A Tragic Grace

A Tragic Grace

The Catholic Church and Child Sexual Abuse

Stephen J. Rossetti

Published in association with the
Interfaith Sexual Trauma Institute,
Collegeville, Minnesota

A Liturgical Press Book

THE LITURGICAL PRESS
Collegeville, Minnesota

Cover design by Greg Becker

1   2   3   4   5   6   7   8

Library of Congress Cataloging-in-Publication Data

Rossetti, Stephen J., 1951–
    A tragic grace : the Catholic Church and child sexual abuse / Stephen J. Rossetti.
            p.   cm.
    "Published in association with the Interfaith Sexual Trauma Institute, Collegeville, Minnesota."
    Includes bibliographical references.
    ISBN 0-8146-2434-0
    1. Catholic Church—Clergy—Sexual behavior.   2. Child sexual abuse by clergy.   I. Interfaith Sexual Trauma Institute (Collegeville, Minn.)   II. Title.
BX1912.9.R67   1996
261.8'32—dc20   96-22804
                                                                    CIP

*This book is dedicated to the memory of Fr. Damian Byrne,
former Master General of the Dominican Order and a major force
behind the development of the Irish sexual abuse policies.*

*He gave much to the universal Church, to Ireland, and to me.
He died on February 18, 1996, less than three weeks after
the Irish document was released. Damian's work was finished.*

I am grateful to God for this humble and holy man.

Contents

Foreword

We welcome this volume that is sponsored by the Interfaith Sexual Trauma Institute. The Institute was created in May 1994 by St. John's Abbey and University in partnership with the ISTI Board to address issues within ministry of sexual abuse, exploitation, and harassment through research, education, and publication. The vision of ISTI is the building of healthy, safe, and trustworthy communities of faith.

In its statement of purpose for the institute, the ISTI Board, with membership from some fifteen Jewish and Christian traditions, strongly affirms the goodness of human sexuality and advocates respectful relationship through the appropriate use of power within communities of all religious traditions. Everyone stands to gain by examining openly together whatever we discover are the issues and by providing the means to confidently promote an informed awareness of our common failure. We must look critically at history, sexuality, human relationships, and our collective struggle to develop sexual meaning.

ISTI believes that human sexuality is sacred; misuse of power underlies all forms of sexual compromise, compromise that violates human dignity and harms individuals and communities both emotionally and spiritually. Healing and restoration are possible for survivors, offenders, and their communities through a complex and painful process. However, truth telling and justice making are integral to change and healing in individuals and institutions.

The goals of ISTI are to

- encourage understanding of sexual misconduct through interdisciplinary seminars, conferences, and seminary instruction;

- develop models of intervention, psychological and spiritual healing, restitution, and recovery of community trust in collaboration with such persons as victims, offenders, religious leaders, and those in the helping professions;
- support the systematic study of and theological reflection on healthy human sexuality and appropriate use of power;
- publish materials regarding victims and healing, offenders and rehabilitation, and spiritual communities and their transformation;
- advance research on sexual abuse, exploitation, harassment, and their prevention;
- collect and disseminate accurate information about issues of sexual misconduct;
- network with other professional organizations and agencies that deal with issues of sexual misconduct.

We welcome comments and suggestions. For information on ISTI programs and resources including the ISTI quarterly newsletter, *The ISTI Sun,* please address correspondence to:

Executive Director
Interfaith Sexual Trauma Institute
St. John's Abbey and University
Collegeville, MN 56321 U.S.A.
Phone: 320-363-3931
Fax: 320-363-2115
e-mail: isti@csbsju.edu
Internet: http://www.osb.org/isti/

Introduction

A New Awareness

In my hometown in the 1950s and 1960s, no one ever heard of child sexual abuse, or if they did, it was never mentioned. We knew about boys and girls falling in love and getting married; we were ignorant of the fact that some might not be attracted to adult members of the opposite sex. At night, we left the cars parked in the driveway with the keys in the ignition and we never, *ever,* locked the doors to our homes.

Two decades later, as a young priest, I was approached by a little girl from our parish school who told me that her older brother had touched her private parts. She was upset. I was sympathetic. I asked her if it was still going on and she said no. A few weeks later I checked on her and she said she was okay. In hindsight, I wish I had done more.

I remember a brother priest who took altar boys to his camp overnight on his day off. It seemed strange; why would he want to do that? I also suspected he was an alcoholic but we had no proof. Finally, I asked one of the altar boys if everything was okay. Was the priest treating him well? The young lad said everything was fine. I wish I had followed my intuition and investigated further.

As I began to learn more about sexual abuse, I was shocked to find out that one out of every three or four girls and half as many young boys, one out of six to eight, are sexually molested by their eighteenth birthday. I was also surprised to learn how devastating sexual contact with a trusted adult can be for a child. Perhaps the most destructive effect is a crippling of the victim's ability to trust.

Responding properly to incidents of child sexual abuse pre-supposes:

- an awareness of the pervasiveness of child sexual abuse,
- a realization of the trauma it causes to victims,
- a recognition of the mental illness that afflicts perpetrators, and
- a sensitivity to the signs of child sexual abuse.

At the time, I responded as best I could, but I was not aware that I should have done more. I think it has been the same with the Church and its response. Much of its malfeasance in responding to cases of child sexual abuse was a result of ignorance, not maliciousness. For our actions, or lack of action, in the past, we can plead ignorance. Now, such protestations are unacceptable. This book offers a new way.

A Message of Hope

The insights contained herein are indeed simple ones. After reading this book, one's first thought might be: "These are obvious things." Unfortunately, past reality suggests that they are not.

The insights offered here are the hard lessons of many years of mistakes, costly mistakes. These mistakes were made again and again by diocese after diocese, from religious order to religious order, from one country to the next.

But the Church has no monopoly on such errors. These costly errors have been made by secular authorities and mental health professionals, too. Perhaps these sorts of mistakes are merely human errors, mistakes commonly made by a flawed human nature.

Embedded in this work is a message of hope and, possibly, even a story of human greatness. We are learning. Things are changing. The word is getting out.

The measure of greatness of our church and of our humanity has not been, nor can it be seen, in its first response to a difficult challenge. Our first response is often amiss, although well intended.

Rather, we tried again and again. We listened to victims and we continue to listen. Their pain touched our pain. We recognized a faintly remembered voice and something within began to change.

As the process unfolded, we began to hear on a different level. We started to see with a new clarity. Only then did we understand what the real challenge was. It was then that we could respond. It was then that these insights seemed so simple.

Indeed, there are many simple ideas in this book. There are many action items to remember. But the real message calls for a change of heart.

We should not enter the road to conversion thinking we know where it will lead; we do not. We simply trust that, wherever it leads, we will be blessed for the journey and better off than when we began.

Let us enter this journey with confidence, trying not to cling too hard to former notions and ways of thinking. We know that something new, something better, is just up ahead.

Chapter One

A Slow Awakening

Confronting Child Sexual Abuse in Society

The first recognition of the prevalence of child sexual abuse in society and its damaging effects on the developing psyche were noted by Sigmund Freud in his paper "Aetiology of Hysteria" in 1896.[1] Freud treated several young women for "hysteria" and found a commonality among them: they had been sexually abused as children by adult men. He formulated what was called his *seduction theory* which stated that all hysterical neuroses are a consequence of early sexual abuse.[2]

Freud said that victims of sexual abuse tend to conceal childhood experiences of abuse. When these memories become conscious, the patient experiences "the most violent sensations" including shame.[3] In 1896, Freud believed that the sexual abuse of children was a widespread phenomenon of which few were aware but that would soon become widely known. He wrote, "It is expected that increased attention to the subject will very soon confirm the great frequency of sexual experiences and sexual activity in childhood."[4]

Freud was prepared to be met with "contradiction and disbelief."[5] In a letter to Wilhelm Fliess, Freud recognized that he was

---

[1]Sigmund Freud, Standard Edition, III, 204.
[2]A. Miller, *Thou Shalt Not Be Aware: Society's Betrayal of the Child* (New York: Meridian Books, 1986) 41.
[3]Sigmund Freud, Standard Edition, III, 204.
[4]Ibid., 205.
[5]Ibid., 220.

accusing fathers of widespread sexual exploitation of children.[6] As predicted, Freud's seduction theory was met with "indignation."[7]

Two years after he published the "Aetiology of Hysteria," Freud recanted. In his September 21, 1897, letter to Fliess, Freud said "I no longer believe" in the seduction theory. He noted, "surely such widespread perversions against children are not very probable."[8]

In 1905, Freud's analysis in *The Case of Dora* ascribes Dora's hysteria not to her real childhood sexual experiences with Herr K. Rather, Freud believed the hysteria resulted from her unconscious and repressed sexual desires for Herr K. and unconscious lesbian feelings for his wife, Frau K.

Freud's theories, according to Miller, have been used to blame victims and to conceal the reality of child sexual abuse and the trauma that it causes. After Freud's downplaying of the seduction theory, women who revealed childhood sexual abuse in psychoanalysis were likely to be told that they were not actually abused by their fathers. Rather, the "memory" is actually a childhood fantasy and a desire for sexual contact with the father.[9]

Miller said, "People don't want to listen [to the truth about child sexual abuse] because they are not yet ready to bear what they will hear."[10] Even Sigmund Freud, whose clinical experience exposed him to the widespread reality of the sexual abuse of children, was not able to accept the truth.

A Period of Limited Awareness

Freud's prediction that "very soon" there would be a widespread awareness of the reality of child sexual abuse was not fulfilled, perhaps, in part, because of his own recanting of his "seduction" theory. Subsequent prevalence rates, for several decades, underestimated the percentage of children being sexually abused.

---

[6]J. M. Masson, *The Complete Letters of Sigmund Freud to Wilhelm Fliess 1887–1904* (Cambridge: Harvard University Press, 1985) 264.

[7]A. Miller, *Thou Shalt Not Be Aware*, 308.

[8]J. M. Masson, *The Complete Letters of Sigmund Freud to Wilhelm Fliess 1887–1904*, 264.

[9]A. Miller, *Thou Shalt Not Be Aware*, 322.

[10]Ibid., 302.

For example, Meiselman, in her review of the literature, noted that many studies cited between one and two reported cases of incest per one million people per year in the United States. She believed that there were more cases of incest than those reported, but there was no way of knowing what those figures would be. However, her tentative conclusions were that "incest as an event occurs in one or two lifetimes out of a hundred."[11]

Not only did studies, during this period, underestimate prevalence rates of sexual abuse, they minimized the extent of psychological trauma caused to the victims. The Kinsey report stated that such sexual advances were "not likely to do the child any appreciable harm if the child's parents do not become disturbed" by the abuse.[12] This observation was affirmed by Gagnon and Simon[13] who said, "The evidence suggests that the long-term consequences of victimization are quite mild" and that the most serious scarring for the victim arises when the parents overreact.

Both Kinsey et al. and Gagnon and Simon wrote that the short-term consequences for the victim are generally ones of fear and fright. Kinsey et al. noted that while 80 percent of the children who had sexual contacts with adults had been frightened or upset, "in most instances the reported fright was nearer the level that children will show when they see insects, spiders. . . ."[14]

Sloane and Karpinski repeated the psychoanalytic interpretation begun by Sigmund Freud: "The 'traumatic' aspect furthermore loses some of its significance when It is realized that the child itself often unconsciously desires the sexual activity and becomes a more or less willing partner in it."[15]

Similarly, Bender and Blau studied sixteen prepubescent children who were admitted to Bellevue Hospital after they had sexual

[11]K. Meiselman, *Incest: A Psychological Study of Causes and Effects with Treatment Recommendations* (San Francisco: Jossey-Bass Publishers, 1978) 31.

[12]A. C. Kinsey, W. B. Pomeroy, C. E. Martin, and P. H. Gebhard, *Sexual Behavior in the Human Female* (Philadelphia: W. B. Saunders Co., 1953) 122.

[13]J. H. Gagnon and W. Simon, *Sexual Encounters Between Adults and Children* (New York: SIECUS Publications, 1970) 13.

[14]Kinsey et al., *Sexual Behavior in the Human Female*, 121.

[15]P. Sloane and E. Karpinski, "Effects of Incest on the Participants," *American Journal of Orthopsychiatry* 12 (1942) 666.

relationships with adults. The authors found the children to be "bold, flaunting and even brazen about the situation." They noted that there were indications in their interviews that "children . . . often play an active or even initiating role" in sexual encounters with the adults. They went so far as to say that the child may sometimes even be considered the seducer rather than the one seduced.[16]

Regarding cases of heterosexual incest with boys, the Kinsey report said that "the cases are so few" as to be negligible. They said that this sort of incest "occurs more frequently in the thinking of clinicians and social workers than it does in actual performance."[17]

The Kinsey report found some cases of preadolescent boys being sexually involved with adult women and more cases of boys being involved with adult males. They were not able to give overall incident rates. They did not state that such contacts were abusive or potentially harmful. Instead, they suggested that such events had a positive meaning: "Older persons are the teachers of younger people in all matters, including the sexual."[18]

This attitude began to change in the late 1970s. Finkelhor said there was a rapid rise in the official reports of child sexual abuse. Along with this rapid rise in reporting sexual abuse came considerable national media coverage. Finkelhor said that it seemed as if the issue of child sexual abuse went from "a level of practically total obscurity to one of extremely high visibility."[19] In reality, the subject had been studied by a few scholars but there was little awareness of the extent of sexual abuse in society or its potentially long-term, harmful effects on the victims.

Meiselman said that the issue of child sexual abuse has been raised in public consciousness because of the "wave of sexual openness that swept over us in the 1960s."[20] In the 1960s, it be-

---

[16]L. Bender and A. Blau, "The Reaction of Children to Sexual Relations with Adults," *The American Journal of Orthopsychiatry* 7 (1937) 500–518.

[17]A. C. Kinsey, W. B. Pomeroy, and C. E. Martin, *Sexual Behavior in the Human Male* (Philadelphia: W. B. Saunders Co., 1948) 558.

[18]Ibid., 167.

[19]D. Finkelhor, "Sexual Abuse: A Sociological Perspective," *Child Abuse and Neglect* 6 (1982) 95.

[20]K. Meiselman, *Incest,* ix.

came acceptable to address the issues of sexuality and child sexual abuse more openly.

Finkelhor believed that child sexual abuse has risen in the public consciousness "not primarily because the true prevalence has increased, as some think, but because it has been championed by . . . the women's movement and the children's protection movement."[21] They have fought for the rights of women and children, including exposing the widespread sexual abuse of children.

Confronting Child Sexual Abuse in the Church: The Case of Reverend Gilbert Gauthe

Like society at large, the Catholic Church has been slow, not only to recognize the prevalence of child sexual abuse in its own ranks, but to realize the degree of trauma it causes to the victims. The problem of Church professionals, usually priests, sexually abusing children began to receive extensive national media coverage in the United States in the mid-1980s. The case that first brought priest-child sexual abuse into the public eye was that of Reverend Gilbert Gauthe, of the Diocese of Lafayette, Louisiana.

Jason Berry, an investigative journalist, followed the case closely and published a series of articles in the widely read Catholic newspaper, the *National Catholic Reporter.* The title of one of Jason Berry's many articles was: "Pedophile priest: study in inept church response."[22] Lawsuits were brought against the Catholic Church in 1983 alleging it failed to respond adequately to incidents of Reverend Gauthe sexually abusing children in his parish. The lawsuits finally were settled for a cumulative total of over ten million dollars.

As more cases of clergy-child sexual abuse became public, three men associated with the Catholic Church were sought out by American bishops for their counsel: Reverend Thomas Doyle, O.P., Ray Mouton, and Reverend Michael Peterson, M.D. Rev. Doyle was an expert in Church law, i.e., canon law, who worked at the Vatican embassy in Washington, D.C. Reverend Peterson was

---

[21]D. Finkelhor, "Sexual Abuse," 95.

[22]J. Berry, "Pedophile priest: study in inept church response," *National Catholic Reporter,* June 7, 1985, pp. 6, 19–21.

president of St. Luke Institute, a hospital that provides residential psychological care for clergy. Ray Mouton was a lawyer in Lafayette, Louisiana.

In June of 1985, the American bishops were scheduled to meet at Collegeville, Minnesota for their semi-annual meeting. Doyle, Mouton, and Peterson collaborated on a ninety-two-page paper which was the first comprehensive attempt to address the issue of clergy-child sexual abuse in the Catholic Church. It did so based on the canonical, civil, and psychological information available at the time. In the document, Ray Mouton wrote:

> The first objective, of which one must never loose (sic) sight, is to maintain, preserve and seek to enhance the credibility of the church as a Christian community. The Church should be presented as a sensitive, caring and responsible entity which gives unquestioned attention and concern to the victims. . . . The church must remain open and avoid the appearance of being under seige (sic) or drawn into battle . . . . cliches such as "no comment" must be cast away. In this sophisticated society a media policy of silence implies either necessary secrecy or coverup.[23]

The report was greeted initially with enthusiasm by some individuals in the Catholic hierarchy. But when the Collegeville meeting took place, it was not the Mouton-Doyle-Peterson group that was invited to brief the bishops. In a personal communication, Reverend Doyle said, "All of a sudden the thing died."

In an affidavit by Msgr. Daniel F. Hoye, then general secretary of the United States Catholic Conference (USCC), he stated that the report "was neither requested by nor presented to the NCCB/USCC." Msgr. Hoye testified that the "report gave short shrift to the ongoing diocesan and NCCB/USCC efforts at prevention of sexual abuse."

He further stated that a "key aspect of the Mouton-Doyle-Peterson report was the proposal that a national 'team' at least supplement, but more often displace, diocesan officials in responding to complaints of sexual abuse on a local level." He

---

[23]T. P. Doyle, R. Mouton, and M. Peterson, "The Problem of Sexual Molestation by Roman Catholic Clergy: Meeting the Problem in a Comprehensive and Responsible Manner." Unpublished manuscript distributed to the American bishops by the authors, 1985, 77, 78–79.

noted that "the authors of the report were rather pointed in their dire predictions of the fiscal disaster for the Church unless such a team were hired." Msgr. Hoye added that one of the three authors of the report "intended to be part of that expert team retained at considerable expense by the NCCB/USCC."[24]

Unfortunately, some of the "dire predictions" have come to pass.

Child Sexual Abuse in Canada

A few years later, the Canadian Catholic Church was affected by accusations of child sexual abuse by clergy and religious. The issue began to make headline news in Canada in 1988–89.

On June 1, 1989, a Royal Commission of Inquiry conducted an investigation of abuse charges at Mount Cashel orphanage in Newfoundland.[25] A number of the Irish Christian Brothers were publicly accused of physically and sexually abusing school boys.

During the same time frame, also in Newfoundland, seven priests of the Archdiocese of St. John's were similarly charged. The archdiocese formed its own commission headed by Gordon Winter, a former lieutenant governor of Newfoundland, and focused its investigation on incidents of priests sexually abusing children.[26]

By August of 1989, twenty-three Canadian priests or religious brothers had been publicly charged with abusing children. The President of the Canadian Conference of Catholic Bishops (CCCB), Archbishop James M. Hayes of Halifax, addressed an open letter to Canadian Catholics.[27] He shared the "shock and pain" he and his fellow bishops felt when priests and religious

[24]Affadavit of Monsignor Daniel F. Hoye. United States District Court for the Southern District of Mississippi. Civil Action No. J87–0114 (B), Juanita Spann et al., v. Father Vance Thorne et al., March 16, 1989.

[25]G. A. Winter, N. P. Kennedy, E. MacNeil, F. G. O'Flaherty, and J. A. Scott, *The Report of the Archdiocesan Commission of Enquiry into the Sexual Abuse of Children by Members of the Clergy*, 3 vols. (Archdiocese of St. John's: Newfoundland, Canada [Winter 1990]) 1:vii.

[26]J. Berry, *Lead Us Not Into Temptation: Catholic Priests and the Sexual Abuse of Children* (New York: Doubleday & Co., 1992) 314.

[27]J. M. Hayes, *A Letter to Canadian Catholics About the Church and Sexual Abuse Cases* (Ottawa, Ontario: Canadian Conference of Catholic Bishops, July 10, 1989) 1–2.

brothers were charged with child sexual abuse. He said clearly that their first concern must be the victims: "First in our compassion must be those who have been sexually abused."

The archbishop was also concerned about the "glare of news media reporting" and the accused being "condemned in the court of public information." Likewise, he was worried that "the more than 11,000 priests in Canada . . . should not be brought under suspicion, ridicule, or judgement because of the sins of a small number."

Later that year, during their annual plenary meeting, the Canadian Bishops issued a press release.[28] They said that the first response to allegations of child sexual abuse by clergy should be handled by each individual diocese. However, they agreed that additional guidelines were needed at the national level. They established an ad hoc committee to put forth these new guidelines. The eight-person-committee was led by Archbishop Roger Ebacher of the Archdiocese of Gatineau-Hull.

In June of 1990, the Archdiocese of St. John's Winter Commission completed and published its three-volume report. It acknowledged that charges of a "cover-up" were made by many. Indeed, "the Commission discovered that the Archdiocesan leadership, did, in fact, have knowledge, since the mid-1970s, of deviant or sexually inappropriate behaviour among some Roman Catholic clergy."[29] The commission also charged that "because the Archbishop did not act vigorously on the complaints and concerns of his priests, parishioners and concerned parents, children continued to be abused by some priests, even while under criminal investigation."[30] Shortly after the publication of the Winter Commission report, the ordinary of St. John's Archdiocese, Archbishop Penney, resigned.[31]

One year after its creation, on November 2, 1990, the CCCB ad hoc Committee on Sexual Abuse announced that they were publishing a study-action booklet that could be used by parish discussion groups. Their intention was to raise consciousness at the most

---

[28]Canadian Conference of Catholic Bishops, *Sexual Abuse and the Church.* Press release. Ottawa, Ontario: Author, November 1, 1989.

[29]Winter et al., *The Report of the Archdiocesan Commission,* 3:2.

[30]Ibid., 1:108.

[31]J. Berry, *Lead Us Not Into Temptation,* 315.

basic level of the Church to the reality of child sexual abuse. The study guide was eventually published in 1992 and was titled: *Breach of Trust Breach of Faith*. The CCCB ad hoc Committee on Sexual Abuse also named four working groups to be led by experts in the appropriate fields. In June of 1992, after collating the findings of the four working groups, the CCCB committee published its report. Their final report was entitled: *From Pain To Hope: Report from the CCCB Ad Hoc Committee on Child Sexual Abuse*. To date, this publication is one of the most comprehensive Catholic documents available to the public regarding child sexual abuse.

Child Sexual Abuse in the United States

In the United States, since the case of Fr. Gilbert Gauthe became known, the problem of clergy involvement in child sexual abuse received increasing national attention. Television talk shows, such as *Donahue*, the *Oprah Winfrey Show*, *Larry King Live*, and *Geraldo* gave national exposure to incidents of priests sexually abusing children.

The widespread publicity surrounding the Gauthe case was surpassed only by the case of a former priest, James Porter, who was accused of sexually molesting over 100 children in Catholic parishes in Massachusetts, New Mexico, and Minnesota.

Porter was criminally charged with molesting a girl who babysat for his family in 1987, the only known incident of abuse by Porter in the State of Minnesota that did *not* fall outside of the statute of limitations. Porter was convicted on December 11, 1992, in Minnesota of six counts of fourth-degree criminal sexual conduct. He received a jail sentence of six months with ten years probation. The judge explained that the long duration of the probationary period was necessary because Porter showed no remorse for what he had done.

When the charges against James Porter became public in May of 1992, the Diocese of Fall River, where Porter had been ordained and served most of his priesthood, responded by making a brief public statement:

> The community of the faithful can trust that this serious matter will be handled with compassion and reverence for all. Since this has become a legal matter, it is not appropriate to comment further.

After that statement was released, for a period of four months, the Diocese of Fall River remained silent.

Larry Grimm, the father of one of Porter's victims, said the Church "hasn't done a thing. They haven't made a very big effort at all."[32] His son echoed his father's dissatisfaction with the Church, "We were not offered help in any way, shape or form. I'm more angry at the church than I am at Porter."[33]

In July of 1992, the *Boston Globe* employed KRC Communications Research of Newton, Massachusetts, to conduct a telephone survey of Massachusetts Catholics and their attitudes about the Catholic Church and child sexual abuse.[34] The survey included 401 men and women interviewed on July 20 and July 21. A large majority, 96 percent, said they were aware of recent news stories of sexual contact between priests and minors.

The survey found that 71 percent of the sample believed that the "church has tried to cover up these kinds of incidents" and that 69 percent did not think that "the church has done enough to address these kinds of incidents."

In August of 1992, Fall River was given a new bishop, Sean O'Malley, a forty-seven-year-old Capuchin friar. As early as June seventeenth, two months before he was installed, he said, "To those who have been victimized, the Catholic community wants to respond to your needs in the best way possible."[35] One Porter victim said, "I think that it's long overdue."[36] The outspoken critic of the Church's handling of the Porter case and legal counsel for most of Porter's victims, Roderick MacLeish, said O'Malley is "on the right track."[37]

In December, 1992, sixty-eight victims of James Porter and the Fall River Diocese announced they had reached a mutual settle-

[32]L. Matchan, "Ex-priest accused in Minnesota," *Boston Globe,* July 14, 1992, pp. 1, 6.

[33]L. Matchan, "Porter admits abusing children as priest, apologizes," *Boston Globe,* July 15, 1992, pp. 1, 29.

[34]J. L. Franklin, "Mass. Catholics fault church on handling of sex charges," *Boston Globe,* July 26, 1992, p. 8.

[35]K. Marachocki, "New bishop offers comforting words," *Boston Herald,* June 17, 1992, p. 24.

[36]D. Aucoin and L. Delgado, "New bishop reaches out to the abused," *Boston Globe,* June 17, 1992, p. 29.

[37]K. Marchocki, "New bishop offers comforting words," p. 24.

ment. Details of the agreement remain secret; however, it was reported that each victim received between $50,000 and $80,000 depending upon the severity of the trauma he or she had suffered.[38] The total settlement figure was estimated to be around five million dollars.

However, before the victims would agree to the monetary arrangement, they insisted that the diocese engage in key reforms. They insisted that a review board including lay members review future diocesan handling of clergy-child sexual abuse cases. They also demanded that the diocese report any future allegations to civil authorities.[39] These demands were agreed upon by Bishop O'Malley and written into the Fall River diocesan policy.

O'Malley was praised by the victims for "doing the right thing."

The U.S. Catholic Hierarchy's Response to Child Sexual Abuse

The United States Catholic Conference (USCC), the administrative body that serves the American bishops, has issued several important short statements regarding child sexual abuse. These statements have helped to set the direction for future Church responses both in the United States and abroad. In 1988, the legal counsel for the USCC, Mr. Mark Chopko, noted that, "Recent years have seen an alarming increase in reported cases of the sexual abuse of children."[40] He recognized that they did not know the scope of the problem: "the USCC has no reliable estimate for either the number of cases or persons involved, other than what is reported." However, the USCC recognized its presence within the Church: "Pedophilia is neither a church nor a clerical problem exclusively, but one affecting religious and secular groups alike."

However, the USCC and its sister organization, the National Conference of Catholic Bishops (NCCB), are only consultative

[38]K. Marchocki, "Alleged Porter victims to get $50G–$80G apiece," *Boston Herald*, December 6, 1992, p. 1.

[39]K. Marchocki, "Million$ awarded sex abuse victims," *Boston Herald*, December 4, 1992, p. 13.

[40]M. E. Chopko, "USCC Pedophilia Statement," *Origins* 17(36) (February 18, 1988) 624.

bodies. As such, they often reiterate that they can merely give suggestions to the 188 individual dioceses in the United States. Therefore, individual dioceses in the United States must respond in their own fashion. Some dioceses have taken direct action to respond swiftly to any allegations raised.

For example, after extensive media coverage of a priest perpetrator of child sexual abuse within the Archdiocese of Seattle, Archbishop Hunthausen addressed a pastoral letter to the people which he asked to "be read from all pulpits on Sunday, 29 May 1988." Apparently, the archbishop felt that this abuse, with its accompanying media coverage, potentially affected everyone in his archdiocese.

The response of the Archdiocese of Chicago has also been one of the most aggressive in the United States. After approximately thirty-four of his priests were accused of sexually molesting children, on October 25, 1991, Cardinal Bernardin convened an independent commission to investigate the problem. The commission's findings were published in June of 1992.[41]

The commission's recommendations not only covered ways of responding to allegations, they also suggested improvements in the screening of future candidates for the priesthood, adding programs in psychosexual education in the seminary curriculum, and scheduling continuing educational programs on child sexual abuse within the archdiocese.

The commission's report is noted for its recommendation of the establishment of an independent review board to oversee the handling of allegations and for its restrictive policy on the return of priest perpetrators to ministry after psychological treatment. Cardinal Bernardin adopted the recommendations of his commission and the resulting archdiocesan policy on sexual abuse has been used as a model for other dioceses.

The first publicized attempt to develop a national Church policy was a one-page statement by the USCC legal counsel, Mark Chopko,[42] in 1988 which was then followed by a similar one-

---

[41]J. Q. Dempsey, J. R. Gorman, J. P. Madden, and A. P. Spilly, *The Cardinal's Commission on Clerical Sexual Misconduct with Minors: Report to Joseph Cardinal Bernardin, Archdiocese of Chicago* (Chicago: Chicago Catholic Publications, June 19, 1992).

[42]M. E. Chopko, "USCC Pedophilia Statement," 624.

page statement released by the Administrative Committee of the National Conference of Catholic Bishops in 1989.[43] They suggested several principles to follow whenever allegations were made. Through repeated restating and releasing of Chopko's and the NCCB statements, the USCC eventually reduced these principles to five:

1. Investigate immediately.
2. Remove the priest whenever the evidence warrants it.
3. Follow the reporting obligations of civil law.
4. Extend pastoral care to the victim and the victim's family.
5. Seek appropriate treatment for the offender.

Chopko stressed that "the Roman Catholic bishops of the United States are deeply committed to addressing such incidents positively."[44] He noted that the bishops began to discuss the problem in 1985 at the Collegeville meeting. It was also discussed by the bishops in 1987. However, by 1988, no documents or statements had yet been made by the bishops.

Again in 1992, the NCCB discussed the problem and another short statement was released by the NCCB president, Archbishop Pilarczyk, in June. This statement was brief but more forceful. He apologized for the mistakes made by the Church in dealing with this issue in the past: "Where lack of understanding and mistakes have added to the pain and hurt of victims and their families, they deserve an apology and we do apologize." But he noted that apologies were not enough: "Far more aggressive steps are needed to protect the innocent, treat the perpetrator, and safeguard our children."[45]

Archbishop Pilarczyk reiterated the five principles previously put out by the NCCB. However, his five principles were slightly different. He combined two principles into one: remove the priest and provide treatment for the offender, and added another: "Within the confines of respect for the privacy of the individuals

[43]National Conference of Catholic Bishops. *Statement on Child Abuse Released by the Administrative Committee* (Washington, D.C., November 5, 1989).

[44]M. E. Chopko, "USCC Pedophilia Statement," 624.

[45]D. Pilarczyk, *Statement of Archbishop Pilarczyk, President of the National Conference of Catholic Bishops, on the Sexual Abuse of Children* (Notre Dame, Ind.: National Conference of Catholic Bishops, June 20, 1992) 2.

involved, deal as openly as possible with members of the community about this incident."[46] After several years of accusations of a Church coverup, the NCCB admitted that such cases should be dealt with more openly.

Mark Chopko wondered, "So why is it that even after these years of sometimes very public and painful struggle, leaders of parish communities still doubt the bishops' commitment or resolve?"[47] In this same letter, Chopko answered his own question, "Part of the answer, I believe, lies in the less than public profile that the bishops deliberately chose while they struggled . . . bishops sometimes chose to say nothing rather than risk saying the wrong thing."

The victims of clergy abuse began to organize. The first major group to form was VOCAL, "Victims of Clergy Abuse Linkup," which changed its name in December of 1992 to "The Linkup." Other victims' groups have formed such as SNAP and the Survivors of Porter. SNAP stands for "Survivors Network for those sexually Abused by Priests" and is based in the Chicago area. The Survivors of Porter include the several scores of adults who were molested as children by James Porter.

When the American bishops convened their annual meeting in Washington, D.C., in November of 1992, the issue of child sexual abuse was *not* on the agenda. Representatives of the Survivors of Porter and VOCAL announced their plans to demonstrate at the conference and to request a meeting with the bishops. Unexpectedly, a group of the bishops agreed to meet with them: Cardinal Mohoney from Los Angeles, Bishop Flynn from Lafayette, Louisiana, and Bishop Quinn from Cleveland.

As a result of this meeting, a resolution was placed before the entire assembly of bishops which reiterated the five principles put forth by Archbishop Daniel E. Pilarczyk in his statement in June. The resolution was passed in November 1992. While the assembly did not promulgate any new statements, this resolution was a step forward in that it was agreed upon by the American bishops as a whole. Previously, statements had come from committees or individuals within the USCC and NCCB. Now, the American bishops, as a group, had begun to face the problem publicly.

[46]Ibid., 3.
[47]M. E. Chopko, Letter to the editor, *Today's Parish,* January 1993, p. 4.

Also, the NCCB convened a "Think Tank" of about thirty experts from the United States and Canada in the field of child sexual abuse. They gathered in St. Louis February 21–23, 1993, to discuss the problem of child sexual abuse as it related to the Catholic Church in the United States. The work of the task force became a document which was sent by the USCC to every bishop in the United States.

The group was clear about its primary message to the American bishops; it was a message of urgency. The opening paragraph said, "It is the clear sense of the 'Think Tank' that the bishops be aware of the urgency which accompanies our recommendations . . . we are concerned that the hierarchy's authority and credibility in the United States is eroding. . . ." Again in the conclusion, "We have developed our recommendations with a sense of urgency for action." The reality of child sexual abuse and the perceived difficulties the Church has in dealing with the problem has resulted, in what the "Think Tank" called, "a sustained crisis."[48]

Based upon the receipt of these recommendations, the National Conference of Catholic Bishops announced in its June 1993 meeting the formation of a new ad hoc committee, headed by Bishop Kinney, formerly of Bismarck, to study the problem. Father Tom Bevan of the Priestly Life and Ministry Committee of the NCCB and Father Everett MacNeil, former general secretary for the CCCB and a commissioner with the Canadian Winter Commission, were important staff members assisting in the work of the ad hoc committee. At the November 1994 and 1995 meetings of U.S. bishops, the committee passed out folders to each bishop which included the results of their work entitled "Restoring Trust."

The binders included several articles on child sexual abuse written for the bishops by experts in the field, samples and commentaries on diocesan policies in the United States on child sexual abuse, and a survey of frequently used evaluation and treatment programs for clergy-perpetrators of sexual abuse. The November 1995 binder included a major article on dealing sensitively with victims. The article contained three victim stories

---

[48] *Recommendations of the "Think Tank" on Child Sexual Abuse, Draft V* (Washington, D.C.: National Conference of Catholic Bishops, 1993).

and recommended a coordinated and pastorally sensitive response to the plight of child sex abuse victims.

It is expected that a third installment of "Restoring Trust" will be given to the United States bishops sometime in 1996. The committee expected that the majority of its work would be finished shortly thereafter. Presumably, it would then be dissolved. It is likely that some of the remaining work on this issue would then be taken up by two NCCB committees: the Committee on Priestly Life and Ministry and the Committee on Vocations and Priestly Formation.

An American Problem?

Vatican officials have made a few public statements on this issue. They have condemned the evil of child sexual abuse. They have called for a better screening of candidates for the priesthood and religious life. They have recognized the truth that, while some clerics have been involved in sexually abusing minors, these offenders are "a small number." In addition, it appears that some of its officials originally viewed it as an American problem.

On June 11, 1993, Pope John Paul II signed a letter to the Catholic bishops of the United States acknowledging "how much you, the Pastors of the Church in the United States, together with all the faithful, are suffering because of certain cases of scandal given by members of the clergy."[49]

During that same month, he gave a speech to some American bishops in which he stressed the importance of screening candidates for the priesthood and including a "healthy psycho-sexual development" in the formation of seminarians. He said, "The failures of a small number of clerics make it all the more important that seminary formation discern scrupulously the charism of celibacy among candidates for the priesthood." The Pope went on to say that this formation of priests must take into account the United States' environment "where a culture of self-centeredness and self-indulgence has made inroads."[50]

[49]Pope John Paul II, "Venerable and Dear Brother Bishops of the United States," Letter, June 11, 1993.
[50]C. Wooden, "U.S. Church Must Do Better Job of Screening Seminarians, Pope Says," *Catholic News Service,* June 8, 1993.

The American bishops asked Vatican officials for the power to be able to laicize forcibly some of these priest-perpetrators. The request was denied by the Vatican. Archbishop Agnelo, secretary for the Congregation for Divine Worship and Sacraments, said that canon law does not allow this power to be exercised by individual bishops. He said, "For now, according to canon law, we can do no more than that."[51] His statement suggested that things might change in the future, but it would take a direct intervention by the Pope.

In the interim, the Pope established a joint committee of experts from the Vatican and the American NCCB to "study how the universal canonical norms can best be applied to the particular situation of the United States." Subsequently, the Vatican, in April of 1994, expanded the criteria under canon law in which penalties could be invoked on priest-perpetrators of child sexual abuse. In addition, in September of 1995, the Vatican's highest court, the Supreme Tribunal of the Apostolic Signature, upheld American Bishop Wuerl's suspension of a priest accused of child molestation. The court allowed the use of canon 1044 to remove a priest-perpetrator from ministry by expanding what is meant by the phrase, "psychic defect." Previously, it had been more narrowly applied to those priests suffering from psychosis. These changes are an initial attempt by the Vatican's legal system to assist bishops in dealing with the problem of clergy who sexually molest minors.

The Vatican spokesman, Joaquin Navarro-Valls, was even more direct in his comments about this being an American problem. He said the phenomenon of priests being involved in child sexual abuse raises serious questions about the moral direction of America. He suggested that the "main defendant" is "a society that is irresponsibly permissive, hyperinflated with sexuality and capable of creating circumstances that can induce into grave moral acts even people who have received for years a solid moral formation and education in virtue."[52]

---

[51] J. Thavis, "Vatican, For Now, Nixes Speedier Laicization for Pedophiles," *Catholic News Service,* March 24, 1993.

[52] J. Thavis, "Vatican Spokesman Says Abuse Raises Questions About U.S. Morals," *Catholic News Service,* June 23, 1993.

The Pope restated his implication that this is an American problem during his 1993 trip to Denver. He briefly mentioned the issue of clergy-child sexual abuse and said, "America needs much prayer, lest it lose its soul."[53]

However, what is becoming increasingly clear is that the problem of the sexual molestation of minors by clergy extends beyond the borders of America.

Clergy Child Sexual Abuse in Ireland

For instance, cases of clergy-child sexual abuse were catapulted into the Irish public consciousness with the case of Reverend Brendan Smyth. He was a Norbertine priest who sexually molested a number of children over a twenty-four-year period. He received a four-year jail sentence in Northern Ireland. Complicating the case were written documents which demonstrated that the Catholic Church in Ireland was aware of his behavior but continued to allow him to minister. Like the infamous Reverend James Porter of the United States, Fr. Smyth was repeatedly sent for psychiatric treatment but was not able to control his sexual desires for children.

The cardinal primate of Ireland, who himself was criticized for not intervening in Smyth's case, said the Church in Ireland was not aware of how compulsive such behavior can be. Fr. Smyth's superior, Abbot Kevin Smith, resigned.

The extensive media coverage of Reverend Smyth precipitated the surfacing of an increasing number of cases of clergy-child sexual abuse in Ireland. While such revelations would be shocking to any group of the faithful, it has been particularly traumatic for the Church in Ireland. This is so because the island is relatively small, has a strong informal communication network, and has been steeped in an obedient Roman Catholicism for centuries.

For example, a few months after the Brendan Smyth case became public, another priest, Fr. Liam Cosgrove, died in a gay sauna in Dublin. He was anointed by two other priests who apparently were patronizing the same sauna. The owner of the es-

---

[53]A. Cowell, "Pope Expounds Stern Guidelines, Warning U.S. Could Lose Its Soul," *New York Times,* August 15, 1993, p. 1.

tablishment was quoted in the paper as saying that Catholic priests made up a significant number of his patrons, second only to lawyers.

A parishioner of Fr. Cosgrove's said he was "a good fellow, a decent Christian man." But she could not understand how Fr. Cosgrove ended up in a gay sauna and said, while shaking her rosary beads at the reporter, "He couldn't have been a homosexual. For chrissakes, Father Liam was a priest!"[54] If the faithful in Ireland have difficulty accepting that a priest could be sexually attracted to another adult male, it must be well-nigh impossible for many of them to believe that a priest could be sexually excited by children.

However, the Catholic Church in Ireland has attempted to learn from the experience in North America. At the beginning of the public outbreak of cases of sexual abuse, the Irish Church enlisted the aid of an American media expert, Carol Stanton. Stanton was a seasoned veteran in dealing with the American media, particularly in cases of clergy sexual misconduct. Also, they sent several Irish clerics, canon lawyers, and civil lawyers to visit the United States to inquire how the "States" had learned to deal with cases of abuse. The U.S. Catholic Conference, several American dioceses including Chicago, and clinical treatment programs such as Saint Luke Institute shared their collective wisdom and experience and provided copies of USCC documents and various diocesan policies.

With the assistance of the untiring efforts of Fr. Damian Byrne, O.P., the executive director of the Conference of Religious in Ireland, the Irish bishops have attempted to respond to allegations of abuse. The cardinal primate of Ireland, Cardinal Daly, publicly promised an open and aggressive handling of future cases and full cooperation with civil authorities.

Even before the Brendan Smyth case became public, Bishop Forristal had been heading a committee to study child sexual abuse for the Irish Bishops Conference. In the wake of the new outbreak of cases, the committee assisted the Irish bishops in releasing statements in June of 1994 and November of 1994. The

[54]"Church confronts sins of fathers in sex scandals," *The News-Journal,* Daytona Beach, Fla., November 19, 1994, p. 10A.

bishops apologized for the misconduct of a few of their priests and they vowed to "address the evil of child abuse."

In its November 1994 statement, the Catholic Bishops of Ireland, with the guidance of Bishop Forristal's committee, apologized for the sexual misconduct of some Irish priests. In their public statement, they said, "They [victims and families] deserve an apology, which we unreservedly offer."

The bishops of Ireland also endorsed several principles in dealing with the problem. They committed themselves to a response that would be *pro-victim;* they said, "The primary concern must be the safety of children." They promised to deal with the problem in an open way: "We fully accept our obligations in regard to the civil law and the need to cooperate with the civil authorities." And they promised to take an active, pastoral role: "We are determined to do all that we can to prevent such behaviour in the future and to offer pastoral care to children and families who have been hurt."

The Forristal committee, in January 1996, released a comprehensive document to assist the Irish Catholic Church in dealing with this problem, entitled, "Child Sexual Abuse: Framework for a Church Response." The document was well received by the media and the Irish Catholic hierarchy.

Taking a Proactive Stance

Clinical journals have documented and studied secular cases of child sexual abuse around the world: e.g., Hong Kong, China, Japan, Greece, Italy, Scotland, Austria, England, Germany, the Philippines, France, South Africa, Denmark, Norway, Sweden, Australia, and Holland.

As it has in Canada, the United States and Ireland, cases of clergy-child sexual abuse have begun to appear publicly in many of the above-named countries. No part of the globe seems to be exempt from the scourge of child sexual abuse. There is no reason to believe that clergy are not also offenders in any country where child sexual abuse occurs.

The public exposure of clergy perpetrators of child sexual abuse that has begun in the Catholic Church in the United States and Canada is spreading, first to English-speaking nations and then, apparently, around the globe. It is unlikely that any region of the Catholic Church will be spared.

One can hope that ecclesiastical authorities in countries where the problem has not yet surfaced will learn from the mistakes and the positive steps made in such countries as Canada, the United States, and Ireland. Even more to the point, rather than waiting for the "wave" of child sexual abuse allegations to hit their countries, local bishops conferences might act proactively.

Bishops' conferences around the world could establish diocesan guidelines for dealing with cases of clergy sexual misconduct, institute more rigorous screening procedures for candidates to the priesthood and religious life, begin programs in healthy sexuality, and announce a proactive public stance condemning child sexual abuse. They would do well to promise the faithful to respond to allegations aggressively and with pastoral sensitivity and to institute such procedures *before* the "wave" of public awareness of child sexual abuse hits them.

Taking such a proactive stance, before allegations of child sexual abuse by clergy have surfaced in one's country, would take a great deal of courage. It would be soundly criticized by many churchmen. Some will assert that child sexual abuse is not a problem in their dioceses. Others will undoubtedly say that such actions would cause unnecessary scandal.

But those bishops who speak proactively about child sexual abuse will be prophetic voices. The scandal that has already occurred was not in the Church's speaking about child sexual abuse; the scandal was in *not speaking* about it, especially when so many suffering and confused people needed to hear the Church's voice.

Vatican Leadership?

If child sexual abuse, perpetrated by clergy, is a world-wide issue, would it not seem appropriate for the Vatican to take a strong, proactive stance as well? The Vatican could play a strong leadership role in raising consciousness around the world to the evil of child sexual abuse and recommending aggressive yet pastoral steps in prevention and treatment. Pope John Paul II has long been an advocate of children. This would be a natural extension of his ministry.

The Vatican could assist national bishops' conferences by collecting and spreading ecclesiastical information on child sexual abuse. It could reform canon law which sometimes functions as a hindrance to a proper church response to clergy perpetrators. The Vatican could be a potent force in assisting Catholic bishops around the world so that they might face the reality of clergy-child sexual abuse with honesty, openness, and alacrity.

The Church Is Waiting

To date, bishops' conferences, religious orders, and dioceses in other parts of the world appear to be waiting. It is as if they are saying, "This is not a problem for us"; and "Our clergy do not do such things." To date, ecclesiastical authorities have not dealt with this painful issue until forced to do so.

Perhaps this should be expected. Secular society struggled, and continues to struggle, to accept the reality and pervasiveness of child sexual abuse. Sigmund Freud himself denied his own original insights regarding this truth.

Each country and each church may have to go through its own process of conversion. The process begins with *denial*. We say, for example, "Child sexual abuse does not happen here." When the initial cases of child abuse surface, there is then a period of attempted *containment*. The approach then becomes: "Keep it quiet; keep it contained."

But after more and more cases surface, the problem becomes impossible to deny or to contain. Then we are given a choice to either change our perspective and to respond willingly or to stay stuck in the old patterns of denial.

It is a painful and expensive process of conversion. It may be unrealistic to expect leaders to address the issue proactively until this process of conversion has been completed. Perhaps all we can hope for is that the time it takes for the conversion process could be shortened and the damages incurred would be minimized.

The problem of clergy perpetration of child sexual abuse has been linked to American society which is "permissive" and "hyperinflated with sexuality." But clergy-child sexual abuse is not simply an American problem. Documentation of child sexual abuse is pouring in from every part of the globe. Just as secular cases of child sexual abuse occur throughout the world, perpe-trators of these crimes inevitably include members of the clergy.

The Pope has warned that America is in danger of "losing its soul." I do not deny that this is so. But if child sexual abuse is a global problem, then it may be that the entire world is in danger of losing its soul.

Eventually, the problem will end up on each diocese's steps. One can act now, taking a prophetic and proactive stance or one can wait until forced to act. Either way, the time will come.

Chapter Two
A Wounded Church

In a New England cable news broadcast, the pictures of two priests being accused of child sexual abuse were displayed. After the pictures, a young mother was interviewed while she tightly held the hand of her five-year-old daughter. Although she resided in a different parish from either of these men, she had taken her daughter out of Sunday school classes and will no longer leave her child in the church alone. She is afraid of what a priest might do.

Clinical research has pointed out the potentially devastating effects of child sexual abuse on the victims. Our first thought is for them. But is the clergy perpetration of sexual abuse doing damage to the larger church community and especially to the parish? What effects is it having on parishioner attitudes toward the priesthood?

While it is easy to guess that clergy-child sexual abuse *is* damaging our Church and that it is negatively affecting our attitudes toward priests, there has been no scientific research to show what the effects might be or how deeply it penetrates into parish life. Therefore, Twenty-Third Publications agreed to sponsor a study investigating this issue in the hopes that it might add to our understanding.

Portions of this chapter first appeared in: "Broken Symbols: Child Sexual Abuse and the Priesthood," *Today's Parish,* September 1992, pp. 9–13, and "A Wounded Church: Child Sexual Abuse and the Catholic Church," *Today's Parish,* October 1992, pp. 9–13.

The Research Project

In 1992, before Bishop Kinney's committee on child sexual abuse began its work, surveys were sent to Catholics in the United States and in Canada randomly selected from the Twenty-Third Publications mailing list. The total sample of 1,810 respondents included 391 sisters, 46 deacons, 10 brothers, 314 priests, and 36 others. There were 1,013 completed surveys returned by lay people. Of this entire group, 86 percent were Americans and 14 percent were Canadians.

The great majority of the lay respondents, 87 percent, were practicing Catholics active in ministry as either volunteers or paid staff. Twelve percent were practicing Catholics not active in ministry and 1 percent were inactive Catholics. *Therefore, these survey results reflect the beliefs of active, lay ministers in the Catholic Church in the United States and Canada.*

Three Groups Compared

The 1,013 lay respondents were placed into three groups depending upon their experience of priests being charged with child sexual abuse. The survey asked if "my diocese has been affected by a case(s) of a priest sexually abusing children" and if "a priest in my parish has been accused." They were placed into the three groups based on their answers to these two questions.

There were 349, or 35 percent of the sample, who answered "no" to both questions; they had not experienced either their diocese being affected or a local priest being accused. These people were placed into group 1.

The majority of the respondents, 545 people, or 55 percent of the sample, stated that their diocese had been affected. However, their own parish priest had not been accused. They were labeled as group 2. And group 3 was composed of 10 percent of the sample, 98 respondents, who had experienced their own parish priest being charged.[1]

---

[1]There were 21 surveys from laity which did not have scorable responses, hence the total number of people in the three groups does not equal the total of 1,013 lay respondents.

Thus, group 1 had the least experience of clergy-child mo-lestation. Group 2 had more exposure and group 3 had the greatest amount. These three groups' responses on a variety of questions were compared to assess the effect of such experiences on Catholics' trust in the priesthood.

Survey Questions

Do you "agree," "disagree," or are "unsure" concerning the following statements?

I expect a priest's moral conduct to be better than other people's conduct.

I look to Catholic priests to provide moral leadership.

When a new priest arrives in our parish, I wonder if he is someone we can trust.

When someone wants to be a priest today, I wonder if he has sexual problems.

Compared to other males in our society, priests are more involved in child abuse.

If I had a child, I would allow him/her to go on vacation with a priest.

If I had a son, I would be pleased if he wanted to be a priest.

If I had a son, I would be pleased if he became an altar-server.

Overall, I am satisfied with the priests that we have in the Church today.

I support the requirement that priests live a celibate life.

The Catholic Church is dealing with the problem of sexual abuse directly.

The Church's current response to the sexual abuse of chil-dren by priests is adequate.

I have been kept adequately informed by the Church about child sexual abuse.   *(Survey continued on next page.)*

(Survey continued from previous page.)

Incidents of priests sexually abusing children should *not* be made public.

I look to the Church to provide guidance on issues of human sexuality.

I trust the Catholic Church to take care of problems with its own clergy.

I would send my child to a Catholic summer camp.

I believe that the Church will safeguard the children entrusted to its care.

Overall, I am satisfied with the Catholic Church today.

People Are Angry

The respondents were asked what emotion they felt when they heard about clergy being involved in child sexual abuse. They responded:

angry 32%	disappointed 17%	ashamed 4%
sad 22%	compassionate 8%	miscellaneous 17%

When asked to describe the strength of this emotion, the overwhelming majority (86 percent) of the sample said it was strong or very strong. *Thus, child sexual abuse by the clergy evokes strong feelings in Catholics: they are very angry, very sad, and very disappointed.*

Priests Should Be Better?

This strong emotional reaction is particularly understandable when one looks at the responses people gave to the following statement: "I expect a priest's moral conduct to be better than other people's conduct." A large majority, 83 percent, said they agreed. *Catholics do expect their priests to be better.*

Indeed, awareness of clergy involvement in child sexual abuse is often resisted by parishioners. Nancy Hopkins, a mental health professional who specializes in clergy misconduct, compared the psychological denial found in clerical cases to that found in other clinical settings:

The denial in clergy sexual misconduct cases seems to be of a deeper and more intractable kind. I think it is impossible to overstate the power that the clerical role exerts on the psyches of many people. Though often irrational and unconscious, the dynamics of projection and transference seem to be every bit as prevalent as with any of the other helping professions. The additional ingredient which drives the other two with so much intensity is the embodiment of the Divine in the person of the ordained.[2]

The reality of clergy sexual misconduct is even resisted by many of the victims. As one survey respondent wrote, "I was fondled by a priest in our school hallway when I was 12 years old. In college, a priest made verbal sexual advances to me. In both cases, I wasn't sure this was *really* happening to me." It is difficult for a child to believe that he or she has been molested by a trusted adult. When the perpetrator is a member of the clergy, the event is all the more incredible.

An Erosion of Confidence

As incidents of clerical child abuse become known, the survey results indicate a corresponding decline in confidence in the priesthood.

For example, those Catholics whose diocese had experienced a priest being accused of child sexual abuse (group 2) were less likely to believe that a priest's conduct should be better than other people's conduct: there was a 2 percent decline. If their own parish priest had been accused, the decline was even greater: it fell 11 percent. With this large sample of 1,013 people, an 11 percent decline was statistically significant and pointed to a substantial drop in public expectations of priests.

There was a similar decline in agreement with the statement, "I look to Catholic priests to provide moral leadership." While the initial support was high, 95 percent agreement, there was a 4 percent decline for group 2 and a 7 percent decline for group 3.

Those who have experienced priests being accused of child molestation are less likely to expect priests to be better than others and they are less likely to look to priests for moral leadership.

[2]Nancy M. Hopkins, "Congregational Intervention When the Pastor has Committed Sexual Misconduct," *Pastoral Psychology* 39(4) (1991) 249.

Table 1

Percent (%) Agreement

	Group 1	Group 2	Group 3
priests conduct better	83	81	72
priests provide leadership	95	91	88

Group 1 = no experience
Group 2 = priest in my diocese accused
Group 3 = priest in my parish accused

A Decline in Trust

The survey presented a number of statements about trust in the priesthood. The good news is that the majority, 59 percent of active Catholics, without an experience of priests being accused of child molestation (group 1), continue to trust new priests assigned to their parish. Similarly, an even larger 81 percent disagreed with the statement, "When someone wants to be a priest today, I wonder if he has sexual problems." Likewise, 73 percent of this same group believed that priests are less involved in child abuse than other adult males in our society. All three are positive signs of trust in the priesthood.

Table 2

Percent (%) Disagreement

	Group 1	Group 2	Group 3
wonder if can trust priests	59	48	44
priests have sexual problems	81	73	58
priests more involved in abuse	73	48	32

Group 1 = no experience
Group 2 = priest in my diocese accused
Group 3 = priest in my parish accused

However, this level of trust decreased substantially for those who had been exposed to the phenomenon of child sexual abuse by priests. They were more likely to wonder if a priest has sexual problems, an 8 percent (group 2) decline and 23 percent (group 3) drop. Also, they were more likely to wonder if he is someone they can trust, an 11 percent and 15 percent decrease for group 2 and group 3 respectively. Similarly, there was a large decrease in those who thought priests were less involved in child abuse than other males in society: from 73 percent (group 1) to 48 percent (group 2) to 32 percent (group 3).[3]

The survey also asked if they would allow a son or a daughter to go on vacation with a priest. For those who had no experience of clergy-child abuse (group 1), 43 percent gave an unqualified "yes." It dropped to 33 percent if a priest in their diocese had been accused (group 2), and fell even farther, to 26 percent, if their own parish priest had been charged (group 3).

Table 3

Percent (%) **Agreement**

child vacation with priest	43	33	26
	Group 1	Group 2	Group 3

Group 1 = no experience
Group 2 = priest in my diocese accused
Group 3 = priest in my parish accused

These data suggest that the more people encounter the phenomenon of clergy-child sexual abuse, the greater the decrease in their trust in the priesthood. For many of the faithful, this decline in trust is particularly distressing. As one Catholic lamented, "If you can't trust a priest, who can you trust?"

---

[3]For those who had experienced a priest as a child molester, there was a significant rise in belief that priests were *more* involved in child sexual abuse than other males in our society: Group 1 = 4%, Group 2 = 10%, and Group 3 = 18%.

Will This Affect Vocations?

It was encouraging to see that the respondents strongly supported priestly vocations. Eighty-one percent of those in group 1 endorsed the statement, "If I had a son, I would be pleased if he wanted to become a priest." Similarly, 92 percent of the same group would be pleased if their son became an altar-server.

These active Catholics demonstrated a willingness to support vocations within their own families.

Table 4

	Percent (%) Agreement		
want son as priest	81	68	57
want son as altar-server	92	87	83
	Group 1	Group 2	Group 3

Group 1 = no experience
Group 2 = priest in my diocese accused
Group 3 = priest in my parish accused

However, this support declined considerably for those who had been subjected to priests as child molesters. There was a 13 percent decline and a large 24 percent drop in endorsement of the statement: "If I had a son, I would be pleased if he wanted to become a priest" for groups 2 and 3. Likewise, there was a 5 percent and 9 percent decline in willingness to have a son become an altar-server in groups 2 and 3.

While support for priestly vocations remains high among active Catholics with little exposure to clergy-child abuse cases, there is a large decline in support among those who have had such an exposure. In addition, the closer a lay minister experiences the sexual abuse of children by the clergy, the greater the reduction in support. Since parental support is considered to be an important factor in the fostering of religious vocations, *there is a strong likelihood that incidents of clergy sexual misconduct will have a negative effect on future vocations.*

Overall Satisfaction Drops Sharply

One of the most disturbing results of this research was found in the respondents' answers to the statement: "Overall, I am satisfied with the priests that we have in the Church today." This survey item is a straightforward measure of people's overall satisfaction with their priests. The initial responses were clearly positive: 69 percent agreed with the statement. This 69 percent approval rate is a strong, positive endorsement.

Table 5

	Percent (%) **Agreement**		
satisfied with priests	69	50	34
	Group 1	Group 2	Group 3

Group 1 = no experience
Group 2 = priest in my diocese accused
Group 3 = priest in my parish accused

However, there was a sharp decline in approval by respondents who had experienced an allegation of clergy-child molestation. Group 2 evidenced a 19 percent decline and group 3 saw a dramatic 35 percent decline in overall satisfaction with the priests in the Church today.

It appears that the sexual misconduct of a single priest has a strong effect on many people's overall satisfaction with priesthood. When a cleric of the diocese is accused, overall support for the priesthood drops sharply from 69 percent to 50 percent. When one's own parish priest is accused, it drops in half. This large decline in support is likely to have a negative effect on future relations between the laity and the clergy in many and unforeseeable ways.

Does Priestly Morale Suffer?

One respondent, a religious woman from Illinois, said, "I was with a large number of priests and when the subject of sexual abuse came up, they were upset, ashamed and embarrassed." Our survey was also completed by 314 American and Canadian priests. This sister's observations were borne out by the results. Priests were less likely than the laity to feel angry and more likely to feel "sad," "ashamed" and "embarrassed."

However, the results did *not* indicate a significant morale problem. Priests overwhelmingly (94 percent) indicated that if they had a son, they would be pleased if he wanted to be a priest. They also strongly supported (96 percent) this "son" being an altar-server.

Likewise, these priests showed a high percentage of satisfaction with fellow priests. Seventy-nine percent agreed with the survey item, "Overall, I am satisfied with the priests we have in the Church today." When presented with an additional survey item, "Overall, I am satisfied with the Catholic Church today," 73 percent of the priests agreed. *These priests appeared to be positive about their vocation and about the Catholic Church.*

These results did not change significantly when priests had become aware of another cleric being accused of child sexual abuse. The only exception, however, was with their support of a "son" becoming a priest. There was a small but statistically significant decline among these priests in wanting a "son" to become a priest if another priest in the same parish had been accused of child molestation. It was a decline of 3 percent.

In addition, there have been indications that priests are becoming wary of expressing affection for children or being alone with them. One respondent, a priest from the Carolinas, wrote:

> I know that as a priest, I bend over backwards to keep from appearing overly interested in a child. I had a kid in my lap Sunday while I was sitting between his mother and grandmother, and when I realized it, I put him down. Scary.

Another respondent, a priest in his thirties from Massachusetts, wrote, "Just the possibility of being accused scares the hell out of me and makes me much colder in my relationships with children." Indeed, there is a danger of people in general, and priests specifically, overreacting to the problem.

A Church Cover-up?

There has been much in the media about the Church's response, or lack thereof, to child sexual abuse by clergy. In the *Philadelphia Inquirer,* Andrew Greeley accused the hierarchy of "still trying to intimidate, stone-wall, bribe and cover up" this issue.[4] In the *National Catholic Reporter,* Jason Berry spoke of an "inept church response."[5] The *Boston Globe* stated that "the Catholic Church is not responding to the problem as aggressively or as uniformly as other religious denominations."[6] Do Catholics agree with these criticisms of the Church, or are such statements isolated examples of "Church-bashing"?

The survey also focused on Catholics' attitudes towards the Church. In particular, it looked at how they perceived the adequacy of the Church's response to clergy-child sexual abuse and what this tragedy has done to their trust in the institutional Church.

Inadequate Church Response

The survey made three statements about the Church's response: (1) "The Catholic Church is dealing with the problem of sexual abuse directly"; (2) "The Church's current response to the sexual abuse of children by priests is adequate"; and (3) "I have been kept adequately informed by the Church about child sexual abuse." The entire sample of 1,810 respondents (1,013 laity, 391 sisters, 46 deacons, 10 brothers, 314 priests, 36 other) were asked if they "agreed," "disagreed," or were "unsure" about these statements.

For each of these three questions, a majority of the respondents *disagreed.* Fifty-one percent did *not* believe that the Church is dealing with the problem directly; 58 percent did *not* believe that the Church's response is adequate; and 62 percent did *not* believe they have been kept adequately informed. As a perma-

[4]Andrew Greeley, *Philadelphia Inquirer,* September 29, 1991.
[5]Jason Berry, "Pedophile priest: study in inept church response," *National Catholic Reporter,* June 7, 1985, pp. 6, 19–21.
[6]Alison Bass, "Some fault church on sex abuse by priests," *Boston Globe,* May 11, 1992, p. 11.

nent deacon in his fifties wrote, "Too many cases are covered up. Bishops must stop protecting priests."

These are particularly important statistics when one recalls that virtually our entire sample was composed of committed Catholic leaders; they were sisters, priests, deacons, brothers, and lay ministers. *Therefore, the majority of the Catholic leadership was dissatisfied with the Church's response to incidents of clergy-child sexual abuse.* They were most dissatisfied with not being kept informed.

Many Catholics shared their frustration with the Church's failure to respond. A priest in his forties from New York State wrote, "I was very angry with the Diocese for trying to deny the problem when I reported it. I was blamed for the 'bad news'—I was the messenger, not the perpetrator." A religious sister in her sixties from the Midwest commented, "In several cases, sisters employed in parishes reported abuse to the local bishop and were ignored and even challenged. How sad!"

The survey then made the statement, "Incidents of priests sexually abusing children should not be made public." A large majority, 70 percent of the entire sample, disagreed with that statement. *It is clear that a majority of ministers in the Catholic Church did not believe that the Church has kept them informed and wanted this problem to be dealt with in a more open manner.* As a priest from Virginia said, "The Church should be more open and not hide it."

Three Groups Compared

The 1,013 lay people in the sample were again taken separately and placed into three aforementioned groups based on the amount of their exposure to priests as perpetrators of child sexual abuse. Group 1 had the least experience of clergy-child molestation, group 2 had more exposure, and group 3 had the greatest amount. The responses of these three groups were compared to study the effects of clergy being accused of child abuse on people's attitudes toward the Church.

Exposure Heightens Dissatisfaction

The groups were first compared on the three questions about the Church's response: Was the Church dealing with the problem

directly? Is the Church's current response to the problem adequate? Have they been kept adequately informed? The effect of
a priest being charged with child molestation is unmistakable.

Table 6			
	Percent (%) **Disagreement**		
Church dealing with problem directly	36	60	70
Church's current response adequate	43	66	80
kept adequately informed	64	71	80
	Group 1	Group 2	Group 3

Sample = 1,013 lay people
Group 1 = no experience
Group 2 = priest in my diocese accused
Group 3 = priest in my parish accused

Only 36 percent of group 1 did not feel the Church is dealing
with the problem directly. This increased dramatically to 60 percent if a priest in their diocese had been accused (group 2), and
rose even higher, to 70 percent, if their own parish priest had
been charged (group 3).

In a similar fashion, only 43 percent of group 1 felt the
Church's response to be inadequate. But this rose quickly to 66
percent for group 2 and then to a large 80 percent for group 3.

For the third question, "kept adequately informed," the respondents of group 1 were stronger in their disagreement. A full
64 percent disagreed, even though they had little firsthand experience of the problem. This dissatisfaction increased even higher
to 71 percent for group 2 and to 80 percent for group 3.

It is clear that the more these lay ministers were exposed to the
problem, the less satisfied they were with the Church's response.
In addition, an overwhelming majority (70–80 percent) of laity
within a parish, whose own priest has been accused, were dissatisfied with how the Church is responding.

This dissatisfaction for group 3 may be indicative of how traumatic it is for an entire parish when its priest has been charged with child sexual abuse. They are in need of pastoral care. In many cases, however, little is being done for them. Often, the priest is whisked away quietly and nothing is ever said.

A lay minister from Pennsylvania complained, "We have had two priests in our parish over the last three years who were here one day, packed and gone the next. No explanation given. Rumors flew."

Confidence in Leadership Declines

The survey made two statements regarding Church leadership: "I look to the Church to provide guidance on issues of human sexuality" and "I trust the Catholic Church to take care of problems with its own clergy."

It is encouraging to note that a full 77 percent of these lay ministers, without an experience of clergy-child abuse, look to the Catholic Church for leadership on sexual issues. However, this decreased by 5 percent for group 2 and dropped 11 percent for group 3. This decline suggests that the Church's credibility as a moral leader is eroding.

Table 7

	Percent (%) Agreement		
Church guidance on sex issues	77	72	66
Church take care of clergy problems	53	33	25
	Group 1	Group 2	Group 3

Sample = 1,013 lay people
Group 1 = no experience
Group 2 = priest in my diocese accused
Group 3 = priest in my parish accused

The responses to the query about "trusting the Church to take care of problems with its own clergy" even more strongly suggested a decline in confidence. A slight majority of group 1, 53 percent, trusted that the Church would take care of problems with its clergy. This level of confidence dropped sharply to 33 percent if a priest in their own diocese had been accused. It fell to less than half of the original figure, to 25 percent, if their own priest had been charged.

Even without an experience of clergy involvement in abuse, lay ministers were ambivalent about the Church's ability to take care of problems with its own clergy. However, after experiencing a priest being accused, only one in four trusted the hierarchy to take care of its problems. *The phenomenon of clergy-child sexual abuse appears to be damaging seriously the credibility of the Catholic Church to police its own ranks.*

Put succinctly by a lay minister in her forties from New York: "I believe the Church is guilty of trying to cover-up any incidents that occur. This is a very serious mistake and the reason why many people don't trust the Church regarding this issue."

Trust Church with Children?

At the outset of this study, I hypothesized that child abuse by a few clergy is affecting people's overall willingness to trust the Church with their children. The survey put forth two questions to determine if this decline in trust could be documented and how much of a drop there would be: (1) "I would send my child to a Catholic summer camp," and (2) "I believe that the Church will safeguard the children entrusted to its care."

The results were significant. Happily, a large percentage of the laity, 78 percent, without an experience of child abuse by clergy, would trust the Church enough to send their child to a Catholic summer camp. But this decreased by 5 percent for those whose diocese has been affected by a case. Moreover, it decreased by a larger 13 percent if their own parish priest has been accused.

It is even more disconcerting to note that the lay ministers in group 1 were ambivalent about the Church protecting its children. Only 50 percent agreed that the Church could be trusted. This dropped sharply to 38 percent for group 2 and almost in

	Percent (%) Agreement		
Table 8			
send child to Catholic camp	78	73	65
Church safeguard children	50	38	28
	Group 1	Group 2	Group 3

Sample = 1,013 lay people
Group 1 = no experience
Group 2 = priest in my diocese accused
Group 3 = priest in my parish accused

half, to 28 percent, for group 3. *After experiencing their own parish priest being charged with child sexual abuse, few trust the Church with their children.*

There are over 7.5 million children in Catholic schools and religious education classes in the United States alone. There is little doubt that incidents of child sexual abuse by clergy are having a significant effect on people's trust in the Church. It is not difficult to imagine how this decline in trust could have serious repercussions on the effectiveness of the Church's ministry to children.

Endorsement of Celibacy Declines

In an effort to understand how a priest could sexually molest a child, many people look to celibacy as a major factor. For example, a recent, front-page article in the *Boston Globe* was entitled, "Sex Cases Put Celibacy Back In Spotlight." However, current research does *not* show any link between celibacy and child sexual abuse.[7] Indeed, most child molesters in our society are, or will be, married. Nevertheless, whenever a sexual problem emerges within the priesthood, celibacy is often cited as the problem.

---

[7]John Bancroft, *Human Sexuality and Its Problems,* 2nd ed. (London: Churchill Livingstone, 1989) 696. "The majority of pedophiles marry at some stage . . . studies have emphasized the problems pedophiles have in establishing satisfactory adult relationships."

I found that many of our survey respondents agreed. A significant number of completed surveys contained comments on celibacy. For example, an active lay minister from New York State wrote, "I believe the cause of sexual abuse by priests is the rule of celibacy." Another respondent, a Catholic in her forties, said, "The celibate life as it is lived out in the Catholic Church leads to unhealthy lifestyles that increase the risk of sexual abuse."

Table 9

	Percent (%) **Agreement**		
support celibacy requirement	32	23	18
	Group 1	Group 2	Group 3

Sample = 1,013 lay people
Group 1 = no experience
Group 2 = priest in my diocese accused
Group 3 = priest in my parish accused

The survey proposed the statement, "I support the requirement that priests live a celibate life." Overall, there was little support for mandatory celibacy: fewer than one-third of the respondents agreed with this statement. For those whose diocese had been affected by a child abuse case, this declined to 23 percent. Support for mandatory celibacy dropped even further, to 18 percent, for those whose parish priest had been accused.

Support for mandatory celibacy, which is already low, is eroded even further by incidents of priests being involved in child sexual abuse.

Satisfaction with Church Plunges

It is heartening to note that a strong majority, 63 percent, of these lay ministers, without an experience of priestly abuse, agreed with the statement, "Overall, I am satisfied with the Catholic Church today." A 63 percent approval rate represents considerable positive support for the Church.

However, it is disturbing that this approval rate dropped so precipitously with exposure to priestly involvement in child sex-

Table 10

Percent (%) **Agreement**

satisfied overall with Church   63   47   34

                      Group 1   Group 2   Group 3

Sample = 1,013 lay people
Group 1 = no experience
Group 2 = priest in my diocese accused
Group 3 = priest in my parish accused

ual abuse. Group 2, those whose diocese has been affected by a case, had a Church approval rate of 47 percent, a substantial drop of 16 percent.

Furthermore, the Church approval rate for Group 3, those whose parish priest had been accused, dropped almost in half. Only 34 percent agreed with the statement, "Overall, I am satisfied with the Catholic Church today." As a married lay woman from Connecticut wrote, "I am more angry with the hierarchy of the Church than with the priests who abuse!"

Given the fact that a person's overall satisfaction with the Church is composed of a variety of factors such as acceptance of Church teachings, the quality of his or her parish life, the charisms of the bishop, and the person's history, this clear and dramatic drop is alarming. A male lay minister in his forties from Canada summarized it well, "This issue and its handling has created more negative feeling and attitude toward the Church itself than any other."

Summary of Results

This survey was completed by 1,810 predominantly active Catholics in the United States and Canada; there were 1,013 who were mostly active lay ministers in their parishes. The results suggest that child sexual abuse by clergy is having a significant and deleterious effect on their attitudes toward the priesthood.[8]

[8]The statistical significances of the data reported in this article were confirmed by using both Pearson product-moment correlation coefficients and an analysis

Laity who knew of a priest accused of child sexual abuse showed a decrease in confidence in priests; their trust in the priesthood declined; their support for priestly vocations and celibacy decreased; and they were much less satisfied with the priests in the Church today.

In addition, these declines were directly related to the proximity of their experience. If the accused priest was in their own parish, the declines in confidence, trust, support, and satisfaction were greater than if the priest was in another parish. *The closer the incident, the greater the harm done.*

The data demonstrated that active lay people's trust, support, satisfaction, and confidence in the priesthood decreased significantly with exposure to the sexual abuse of children by clergy. In addition, the data showed a similar detrimental effect on their attitudes towards the Catholic Church.[9]

People who knew of a priest charged with child sexual abuse were less likely to trust the Church with their children; they had less confidence in the Church to take care of problems with its clergy; they were less supportive of celibacy; and they were less likely to look to the Church for guidance on sexual issues. Moreover, their satisfaction with the Church dropped sharply.

It is of particular significance that the majority of the entire sample of 1,810 Catholic leaders disapproved of the Church's response to the problem. They did not think it was adequate; they did not believe that the Church is facing the problem directly; and they did not feel that they have been kept adequately informed. A large majority favored a more direct and open confrontation of the problem.

---

of variance (ANOVA). For each of the eight survey items reported for the laity, all the correlation coefficients were statistically significant at the .001 level when correlated with their experience of priests being involved in child sexual abuse. For the F values of the anova's run on each of these same eight survey items comparing group 1, group 2, and group 3, the F values were significant at the .002 level or better. The only exception was the item, "I look to the Church to provide guidance on issues of human sexuality." The correlation coefficient and F value were significant at the .004 and .034 levels respectively. Thus, the data reported in this article met a high standard of statistical significance.

[9]Jerry Filteau, "Bishops spend day on problem of child sex abuse by priests," *The Florida Catholic,* June 26, 1992, p. A4.

Sounding an Alarm

Most importantly, the clarity, consistency and strength of these results should sound an alarm throughout the Church. Every item on the survey that measured attitudes toward the priesthood demonstrated a significant decline with respect to incidents of clergy-child sexual abuse. In addition, these reductions were not small; in some cases, they were reduced by half.

Also, trust and confidence in the priesthood are complex psychic phenomena affected by a multitude of factors such as one's personal history and enduring personality traits. The fact that only one variable, one's experience of priests being accused of child sexual abuse, was associated with these declines and the fact that it was demonstrated by a simple, paper-and-pencil instrument, makes the declines all the more significant. In short, the extent of the erosion in confidence, trust, support, and satisfaction with the priesthood documented by this study should be cause for considerable concern.

One of the respondents, a lay minister from Indiana, summarized it well when she wrote:

> These kinds of personal sins have a dramatic impact on the community of the Church, both in the immediate parish or diocese and in the wider Church. There must be some means for community expression and reconciliation when the incidents occur and are made public.

The Catholic Church has taken many strides in responding to the hurt and pain experienced by the victims of child sexual abuse and their families. This research suggests the need to extend our healing ministry beyond the immediate victims to the entire Church, particularly to those parish communities whose own priests have been accused. Indeed, it is not just the victims and their families who have been harmed by these incidents of clergy-child sexual abuse, *the entire community has been wounded.*

Concluding Remarks

A laywoman from Pennsylvania captured a significant finding of this study when she wrote, "The Church needs to learn that her credibility depends on truth and justice. . . . It is OK for the Church to admit her imperfections, seek forgiveness and reconcile herself to the People of God." In some places, this has begun. Cardinal Bernardin wrote to his priests and said, "Frankly, we have made some mistakes."[10] In addition, he publicly apologized to the people of St. Odilo's parish for assigning a known child molester as its pastor.[11]

Some survey respondents saw signs that the Church is beginning to act. A married woman in her forties noted, "I do feel the Church is taking more steps." A lay minister from Ohio wrote, "I applaud the efforts of Bernardin in Chicago." A Minnesota priest said, "Our diocese has taken prompt action and made tremendous strides." A lay minister from Canada said, "I am pleased the CCCB has issued a fairly open statement on this issue."

If we do fulfill our prophetic mission in addressing the evil which is child sexual abuse, even this tragedy may become a source of grace. A priest from Canada shared his experience:

> I have brought priest-sex-abusers to prison, counseled them in and out of prison. I have dealt extensively with victims as well. I am doing so presently. I have learned a great deal in my work with abusers and victims. It has made me a more prayerful and dedicated and caring priest. I have been blessed in many ways.

[10]Joseph Cardinal Bernardin, Unpublished letter to the priests of the Archdiocese (Archdiocese of Chicago, October 25, 1991).

[11]Bob Olmstead, "Cardinal apologizes to parish for abuse case," *National Catholic Register,* November 17, 1991, p. 1.

Chapter Three

Parishes as Victims of Child Sexual Abuse

A short while ago I was in a parish whose pastor was publicly charged with sexually abusing a thirteen-year-old boy. The boy, now a young man, revealed details of an alleged four-year relationship that started with overnights to the priest's camp, lavish gifts, and wrestling. Three years later it progressed to genital fondling and mutual masturbation.

The priest stated publicly that he is innocent. He claimed the alleged victim is emotionally unstable and out to ruin his priesthood. The statute of limitations has run out on possible criminal charges but a civil suit is pending. The young man desires a monetary compensation for the trauma that he believes he has suffered.

The media have been reporting every detail of the confrontation between the alleged perpetrator and the accuser. The priest's parish has gone into shock. The pastor was, and still is, deeply loved by the people. His ten years in the parish were filled with many acts of kindness and pastoral sensitivity. Parishioners cannot reconcile the good that he has done with the charge that he was sexually involved with a young boy. They are divided between feelings of affection for the pastor and feelings of disgust and disappointment.

This internal conflict is emotionally paralyzing and many parishioners are feeling increasingly helpless. They are looking for assistance but their pastor is on administrative leave and the

Portions of this chapter were excerpted from an article by Stephen J. Rossetti in *Human Development Magazine* 4(14) (Winter 1993) 15–20.

recently appointed temporary administrator is reluctant to take any action. Diocesan lawyers have counseled the bishop against going to the parish and releasing any information; they have recommended he remain silent for the duration of the legal proceedings. Rumors are flying in the parish and throughout the diocese. For example, someone heard that there are many other victims who have come forward but have not gone public.

Parishioners are becoming very angry. Some are angry at the pastor; they believe he is guilty and they feel betrayed. Others are angry at the alleged victim for bringing up charges; the victim and his family are being ostracized from the parish. Many are angry at the media for the sensational way the story has been covered. Everyone is angry at the bishop; they believe he has deserted them in their hour of need. And nobody in the parish knows what is happening.

This scenario is being repeated in scores of parishes throughout the United States. As allegations of priest-child sexual abuse begin to surface in other countries, as they already have, similar disastrous events are taking place around the globe.

Increasing Awareness of Trauma to Parishes

I know of concerned chancery officials who have telephoned new parish administrators in the wake of allegations of clerical sexual misconduct and were told that the parish is "fine." Similarly, the Winter Commission, which investigated sexual abuse of children by clergy in Newfoundland, found that some Catholic officials denied that harm had come to the parishes whose pastor had been charged.

But the commission's report refuted such claims: "In certain instances, the view was expressed that the scandal had not had any direct impact on parishioners. This stance, maintained by some clergy and parish officials, is contrary to the evidence provided by individual lay women and men."[1] When the parishioners feel safe enough to vent their feelings, the trauma emerges.

---

[1]G. Winter, N. Kenny, E. MacNeil, F. O'Flaherty, and J. Scott, *The Report of the Archdiocesan Commission of Enquiry into the Sexual Abuse of Children by Members of the Clergy* (St. John's, Newfoundland: Archdiocese of St. John's, 1990) 1:124.

In Chicago, Cardinal Bernardin's Commission on Child Sexual Abuse found that incidents of clergy sexual misconduct had a negative impact on parishioners. Its report said that "incidents of sexual misconduct with minors, when they become known, also have a severely negative impact on the parish communities where priests have served."[2]

The Canadian bishops' document pointed out that it is important to intervene in affected parishes. One of the recommendations of *From Pain to Hope* is to "manifest particular pastoral care for the suffering of the parish community when one of its priests is accused or convicted of child sexual abuse."[3]

Nancy Hopkins, who has worked with Protestant parishes with similar problems, emphasized the importance of early intervention. She noted, "Intervention with the congregation is, therefore, as crucial as with the primary victims, the pastor, and his family."[4] In the same article, Hopkins made an even stronger assertion: "I am convinced that to do nothing with the congregation is to invite the forces of darkness to take over."[5]

The Traumatic Effects on Parishes

A parish whose pastor has been charged with child sexual abuse is almost always divided. There will be divisions in the parish leadership. There will be divisions and conflicts within the parish itself.

Some parishioners who have personally been affected by sexual abuse in their own family may react very strongly; the allegations will reopen old wounds.

For others, the pastor has been a source of blessing for them: he may have visited them when they were sick or baptized their children. These people are more likely to receive the allegations with incredulity.

[2]J. Q. Dempsey, J. R. Gorman, J. P. Madden, and A. P. Spilly, *The Cardinal's Commission on Clerical Sexual Misconduct With Minors: Report to Joseph Cardinal Bernardin, Archdiocese of Chicago* (Chicago: Chicago Catholic Publications, 1992) 7.

[3]*From Pain to Hope*, 50.

[4]Nancy Hopkins, "Congregational Intervention When the Pastor has Committed Sexual Misconduct," *Pastoral Psychology* 39(4) (1991) 247.

[5]Ibid., 251.

People's responses will be affected by a number of factors including their relationship to the priest and their feelings about the priesthood in general. Parishioners who have become part of the priest's inner circle will react differently than the occasional churchgoer who cannot remember the pastor's name. Similarly, parishioners who have come to revere the priesthood and the Catholic Church will respond very differently than others who have become embittered in their religion.

Parishioners' reactions will also be affected by their stage of faith development. For theorist James Fowler, those who are in the earlier stages of faith development, a "conventional" faith, have difficulty distinguishing symbols of the divine, such as the priesthood, with the divine itself. For these people, religious symbols "are not separable from the what they symbolize."[6] Therefore, they will expect a priest to be a uniquely holy person and they will not be able to entertain the notion that he may have sexually abused a child.

People in the earlier stages of faith development are especially likely to have emotional and spiritual needs for the pastor to be innocent. They may be the most vociferous in claiming that the priest has been unjustly accused. To accept that the allegations might be true precipitates an internal crisis in them that challenges their underlying spiritual and psychological beliefs. This is a particularly vulnerable group and requires special, patient attention. Some of these may become so disillusioned that they end up leaving the Catholic Church altogether.

A few other parishioners will be in Fowler's later stages. They have already come to recognize that divine symbols point to God but are not divine in themselves. Therefore, they accept that a priest can be a source of grace and a channel to the divine, yet have very human faults, including the illness of pedophilia. For this group, the allegations will still be upsetting, but less likely to precipitate a crisis of faith.

The emotions of parishioners in affected parishes will run the gamut from anger, disappointment, disgust, betrayal, disbelief, and shock to sadness, grief, and compassion.

---

[6]James W. Fowler, *Stages of Faith: The Psychology of Human Development and the Quest for Meaning* (New York: Harper & Row, 1981) 163.

Long-Term Effects

Some of the possible long-term effects have been documented in the survey results presented in the previous chapter. In the wake of clerical-child sexual abuse, parishioners are more suspecting of priests. They are more likely to wonder if he has sexual problems or if they can trust him. They are less trusting of the Church with their children. They are less trusting of the Church to take care of problems with its clergy. They are less likely to look to the priesthood or to the Church for moral leadership, especially on issues of sexuality. Their support for celibacy drops and they are less likely to encourage a priestly vocation in their own children.

Perhaps most surprising is the drop in overall satisfaction with the priesthood and the Catholic Church. When the laity are not aware of any cases of priest-child sexual abuse, their overall support is relatively high (63–69 percent). But when their own pastor is charged, it drops almost in half (34 percent)!

The survey data demonstrate that, when a priest is charged with child sexual abuse, the resulting erosion of trust and confidence in the priesthood and Church occurs throughout the diocese. *The data also show that the harm is most acute in the parish where the priest was assigned.*

The Catholic priest continues to exercise a pivotal role in the life of a parish community. If he exercises his pastorate well, he is a blessing for the people. If he has significant personal problems that lead to scandal, the effects can be devastating.

The Second Injury

There are several significant factors that affect how traumatic an incident of sexual abuse will be for a victim. The longer the duration of the abuse and the more aggression that is used, the more traumatic the abuse is likely to be. Moreover, abuse by fathers or trusted father-figures has been shown to cause more serious psychic damage in victims than with other types of perpetrators.[7]

---

[7]Angela Browne and David Finkelhor, "Initial and Long-Term Effects: A Review of the Research," in D. Finkelhor et al., *A Sourcebook on Child Sexual Abuse* (Beverly Hills: Sage Publications) 143–179. It is likely that a priest in whom the victim

And it has been shown that the reaction of the people to whom the victim first reveals the abuse is similarly important.

In his summary of the research, Finkelhor concluded that "negative parental reactions serve to aggravate trauma in sexually abused children."[8] If the victim feels ignored or, even worse, blamed for the abuse, a phenomenon sometimes called "the second injury" is likely to occur. The original acts of sexual abuse cause the "first injury." The negative effects of the victim being ignored or blamed exacerbate the original trauma and inflict the "second injury."

When a pastor is charged with child sexual abuse, his parish responds as a victim does. It, too, has been traumatized and needs a sympathetic ear. If an affected parish's trauma is ignored or if they are blamed for the abuse, it will suffer the "second injury." In addition to being upset by the pastor's alleged actions, parishioners are traumatized by the lack of manifest concern for their pain.

My survey data, as noted in the previous chapter, suggest that affected parishes have been suffering such a "second injury." Many active Catholics did not believe the Church is dealing with the problem of sexual abuse directly, nor did they feel the Church's current response is adequate, and they did not feel they have been kept adequately informed.

It was striking how strong the negative sentiment was among those who had some firsthand experience of a priest in their diocese being charged. The majority (60–71 percent) of those who knew of a priest in their diocese who had been accused were dissatisfied with the Church support they received in the wake of allegations. This dissatisfaction was even stronger among those whose own pastor had been accused; fully 70 to 80 percent of them did not feel that the Church had responded adequately to their needs. It is likely that they suffered the "second injury." Privately, many have confided that they felt abandoned.

In our survey responses, I found that people were angry and disappointed with the priests who had molested young children.

---

and/or the victim's family trusts would fall into the Finkelhor's category of "father-figure." Thus, abuse by a priest would likely be especially traumatic.

[8]Ibid., 174.

Catholics, like their peers in society, acknowledge child sexual abuse as a heinous crime. But an equal source of disappointment and anger was the perceived lack of responsiveness by the Church. As one Catholic said, "I'm more angry at the church than I am at [the priest]."

Parishes suffer deeply when their pastors are charged with sexual misconduct. Whether they are able to reveal it to inquiring Church officials or not, or whether they are fully conscious of it or not, parishes need help, and they need it quickly.

Parishioners Want Information

First of all, people want and need information. Many times, they receive little from Church officials or the parish leadership. The diocesan response to inquiries is often "No comment" or a brief statement. To obtain information, parishioners are forced to rely on rumors and the secular media.

Many times diocesan attorneys recommend that Church officials say nothing while civil and/or criminal proceedings are possible or underway. This may be good legal advice but it cripples the pastoral leadership that the bishop should exercise in a crisis. Mark Chopko, the NCCB's general counsel, recognized this problem, "The defense bar has sometimes dissuaded bishops from acting like the pastors they are, for fear of appearing to admit liability."[9] The November 1992 resolution passed by the American bishops recognized the people's need for information, "Within the confines of respect for the privacy of the individuals involved, deal as openly as possible with members of the community."

Diocesan leaders cannot reveal information that would prejudice legal proceedings nor can they speak of confidential details that rightfully remain private. Nevertheless, there is much that can be spoken by Church leaders to stop destructive rumors, to correct false impressions given by secular sources, and to allay unreasonable fears. Using both legal and pastoral advice, it is possible for diocesan leaders to chart a course of action that is

[9]Mark Chopko, "Restoring Trust and Faith," in *A Brief Overview of Conference Involvement in Assisting Dioceses With Child Molestation Claims* (Washington, D.C.: NCCB's Ad Hoc Committee on Sexual Abuse, September 1993) 41.

legally prudent yet pastorally sensitive to the needs of affected Catholic communities.

Parishioners who are forced to rely on the secular media for information often receive a superficial and sensational understanding of the Church's response. It is difficult for the media to present the complexities of these cases. The secular media reinforce the parishioners' feelings that the Church is covering up the problem and has abandoned them.

When a priest has been charged with sexual misconduct, parishioners want and need information, and they need to hear it directly from Church officials.

Authoritative Presence Required

In addition to the need for information, parishioners whose pastor has been publicly charged with child sexual abuse need strong leadership. In most cases, an accused pastor will be temporarily removed from his pastorate and placed on administrative leave. The absence of leadership and the rumors of allegations of misconduct create confusion and turmoil. In such a crisis, the need for leadership becomes acute.

Chancery officials may be reluctant to intervene in such parishes. They often do not know how to help the parish. They might be aware the parish is struggling, but they often feel inadequate to the task. Chancery officials have sometimes said, "If the parish wants our help, they will ask." In addition, as noted previously, diocesan attorneys may be advocating silence.

On the other hand, parishes may not ask for help from the chancery but usually expect an offer to be forthcoming. When the offer is not made, there is considerable resentment ("Why didn't they come to help us? They must not care about us, or they simply can't face the problem").

As a result, the parish is left in a leadership vacuum. The members of the parish leadership are sharply divided and confused, and they are likely to focus their anger on the diocese. If a temporary administrator is moved into the parish, he or she can be of some help. But what people want is for the bishop and his staff to be a direct, concrete presence during this difficult time. The people's need for leadership is clear, and they expect the hierarchy to respond.

It is understandable that one's natural inclination would be to shy away from the painful task of discussing clerical sexual misconduct with the perpetrator's parish. But people want to know the steps that are being taken by the diocese. They want to know that their anger, confusion, and pain are heard. They want to know that, at this critical moment, the bishop personally is in charge.

Some bishops have made announcements from the parish pulpit. Others have offered a Mass of healing in the parish. Still others have sent personal messages via an episcopal vicar.

In the early stages, a bishop may have few answers or can say little. However, his authoritative presence communicates the most important message: he is concerned with the parishioners' pain and wants to help.

Healing Always Needed

This chapter has outlined the need for *information* and for *leadership* in victimized parishes. There is a third and obvious need: the need for healing.

Some time ago I went to a parish whose pastor had been charged with sexually abusing several adolescent boys. The cases had gone to trial in a civil suit and were eventually settled out of court. The priest was sent into treatment.

During the first night we gathered, there was the usual anger at the priest and the diocese. Many asked, "How could the diocese send in a priest when there had been rumors that something was wrong with him in his previous parish?" Some defended the priest and said that he had done a lot of good. A few wondered if he really was guilty; they distrusted the legal system. There was an undercurrent of guilt, especially among the parents; they wondered if they were not somehow to blame for what had taken place.

The parish leadership complained that the congregation had become dysfunctional. People did not trust the diocese or its new priests. It was difficult to find volunteers for parish projects. Many had become uncooperative and cynical. The parish was splintering into different groups and some had simply left.

The odd thing was that the priest-perpetrator had been charged and had left the parish almost *ten years ago*. The subject of what had taken place had never been raised. For a number of reasons, the new priests and the diocese had never been able to address the issue. Because it had not been addressed, the trauma did not go away, not even after ten years. Rather, it became like a cancer eating away the vitality of the parish.

As noted previously, decades ago many people believed that children who were subject to sexual abuse would "forget." If there was some short-term upset, this would quickly pass. Pastoral experience and clinical research have proven otherwise. It is the same with victimized parishes. The pain and hurt do not go away unless a healing touch is brought to the wound.

There are several persons who need healing in the wake of clergy-child sexual abuse. First and foremost, the children who were victimized are in need of our immediate solicitude. In June of 1992, as president of the NCCB, Archbishop Pilarczyk said, "The protection of the child is and will continue to be our first concern."

The victim's family members may also need assistance. They will be grappling with how to understand what has happened. The pain and trauma caused by such events has split apart even healthy families. With assistance, this need not occur.

In addition to the victim and the victim's family, the church must be concerned about the perpetrator. There is little doubt that perpetrators are suffering from some type of mental dysfunction. While the moral and legal consequences of his actions cannot be ignored, the offender is in need of healing.

The alleged abuser might also be offered pastoral assistance from the diocese. More than one priest has either committed or attempted suicide after allegations have arisen. A priest-mentor and/or mental health professional could provide ongoing support when allegations surface. Most often, the accused longs for direct contact with an understanding and compassionate bishop or religious superior.

As the Church is slowly learning about child sexual abuse and the devastation it causes both victims and their families, Church officials are becoming more effective in dealing with the victims, the victims' families, and the perpetrators. While the media still broadcast news of the failures, many more cases are being successfully handled.

But what is only now emerging is a general appreciation of the need for an *action plan* on how to help parishes after their priests have been charged. Diagram 1 depicts the widening circle of devastation caused by clerical sexual misconduct. The ripples extend far beyond the injured child and family. It must be recognized that the parish and the wider Church are also victims.

Diagram 1

Victims of Clerical Sexual Misconduct

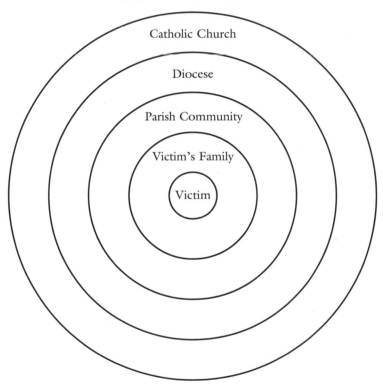

Action Plan for Parishes

This chapter points out the short-term and long-term trauma caused to parishes when their clergy have been charged with sexual misconduct with minors. In particular, it documents the resulting decline in trust and confidence in the priesthood and Church among active Catholics. Contrary to popular wisdom, I do not believe that this erosion of trust and confidence must necessarily follow incidents of clergy sexual misconduct.

If Church leadership took an aggressive, direct, and open response to the problem, I believe it would affirm the Church's spiritual leadership in the minds of the people. They would perceive the mental illness that spawns pedophilia and ephebophilia as an exceptional occurrence in an otherwise healthy and concerned presbyterate. This could turn a crisis of confidence into an affirmation of support.

This aggressive action plan must necessarily include an action plan for parishes. The needs of the parishes, previously mentioned in this chapter, include (1) information, (2) an authoritative presence, and (3) healing. The bishop or his designed representative can be that necessary authoritative presence to the affected parish. To provide additional information and to begin the healing process, the diocese may want to make available the services of qualified and trained pastoral, psychological, and legal professionals.

Parish Assistance Team

A small team of professionals at the diocesan level should be trained and be "on call." This team might include a public relations person, a mental health professional, a civil lawyer, and a pastoral person. Whenever a situation of clerical misconduct arises, chancery officials would contact the parish and ask the leadership if they would like the assistance of this team.

The public relations person would help the parish leadership deal with the media, which may deluge the parish with requests for statements and interviews. He or she might assist the parish leadership in drafting a public statement and in identifying one member of the parish leadership to interact with the media.

The mental health professional and pastoral person might hold listening sessions or parish meetings. They would schedule educational programs to provide information on child sexual abuse. They would help the parishioners process their hurt, anger, and disappointment. They would also make referrals to psychotherapists and pastoral counselors when indicated. For example, public allegations of clerical-child sexual abuse may stir up old wounds in parishioners who themselves were sexually abused in childhood; they should be referred to a mental health professional. In addition to the public relations and mental health professionals, the Parish Assistance Team should include a civil lawyer if the accused priest were to be brought up on civil or criminal charges. The lawyer would provide general information to the parishioners on the legal process and any discussable information related to the case.

Parish Assistance Teams are already in place in a few dioceses. It has been edifying to discover that many fine professionals are willing to donate their time for such service. They only need to be asked!

For example, under Bishop Marshall's personal guidance, the Diocese of Springfield has established a Parish Reconciliation/ Healing Team and outlined procedures for the team to follow when intervening in affected parishes. When a public allegation occurs, the bishop activates the team to lead the parish in the process of healing.

The Diocese of Springfield's written policy stresses the need for a swift response. The policy states, "It is imperative, therefore, that a process of reconciliation and healing be initiated as soon as possible" and "The Parish Reconciliation/Healing Team should meet without delay."

Empowering Parish Leadership

The Springfield policy includes an important realization: "The Parish Reconciliation/Healing Team begins the process of healing and aids the parish leadership in continuing and maintaining this process." The Parish Assistance Team is not designed to take over the leadership of the parish. Rather, its task is to provide necessary professional help at a critical moment. But the ultimate goal is to empower parish leadership to take charge of its own healing process.

Victims of child sexual abuse suffer in many ways. One of the most debilitating effects is often an enduring sense of helplessness. Through their victimization, these children may come to believe that they are powerless and cannot defend themselves. This is one of the reasons why victims of child sexual abuse are at greater risk for being abused as adults. They were "taught" to be passive, powerless victims and continue in this role until an intervention in their life teaches them otherwise.

It is the same with victimized parishes. The parish mentioned previously, whose pastor had been charged with sexual misconduct ten years ago, was not able to move out of its stance of learned helplessness. They remained in this stance for ten years, waiting for someone to come from the outside to help them.

The process that I used with this and other affected parishes is first to meet in a one-day session with the parish leadership including the parish council and parish staff. After allowing them an opportunity to vent their feelings, we work together to establish a series of goals and objectives on how they plan to deal with this crisis. After this session with the leadership, educational and interactive sessions are scheduled with the wider parish.

My goal is to assist affected parishes in recognizing that they can shake off the role of helpless victim and can work together in designing and implementing their own healing process. Once they are so empowered, the parish is well on its way to a stronger and healthier future.

As one Canadian sister wrote in her survey response:

> Our pastor was convicted of sexually abusing boys. Our parishioners were compassionate and understanding of his weakness. It was edifying, and it brought our parish together in prayer for him and for his victims.

Competing Rights

A difficult situation arises when the allegations of sexual misconduct have not been made public. The pastor has been placed on administrative leave and perhaps is undergoing psychological evaluation. The allegations appear to be founded but have not been substantiated in a court of law. Should the diocese make a public statement?

Parishioners are aware that something unusual is happening. The priest usually leaves the parish suddenly and may have told people that he is leaving because of "medical reasons" or for "personal reasons." Members of the parish suspect there is something amiss.

There is no obvious right answer to the question of making the allegations public because there are a number of competing and contradictory rights. Canon 220 states: "No one is permitted to damage unlawfully the good reputation which another person enjoys nor to violate the right of another to protect his or her privacy." This canon recognizes the right of each person to privacy and to a good reputation. One could argue that it is the accused priest's right that allegations remain confidential and not be revealed by Church authorities.

However, the priest's right to privacy and a good reputation are not absolute. The good of the Church can supersede the rights of the individual person. Canon 383 states, "In the exercise of his pastoral office, a diocesan bishop is to show he is concerned with all the Christian faithful who are committed to his care. . . ." One might argue that it is ultimately for the good of the parish community and for the healing of other victims that the allegations become public knowledge.

Canon 220 includes the phrase "to damage unlawfully." It could be argued that revealing allegations of clerical sexual misconduct is not "unlawfully" damaging the priest's reputation since the common good may require it. In addition, if the priest has done something illegal and immoral, i.e., sexually abused a minor, one may reason that his right to privacy and a good reputation are mitigated by this transgression.[10]

Canon 220 applies to all Christians. It should be added that the priest has the additional responsibility of performing a public ministry in the Church. As a public figure given a sacred trust, one might reason that the parish community has a special right to know about substantial violations of the trust they have put in

---

[10]My thanks to Rev. John Beal, J.C.D., for his advice on the application of canon law.

him. Do they not have a right to know why their spiritual leader has suddenly left?

If the diocesan leadership makes a public announcement of the allegations of clerical sexual misconduct, perhaps some people will be scandalized by the allegations who otherwise would not have been. But if no announcement is made, the parishioners will wonder what is happening, they may feel uncared for by the diocese, and rumors will circulate.

In the final analysis, unfounded rumors may be more damaging to the priest's reputation and the spiritual life of the parish than directly and honestly revealing the truth.

Allegations Sometimes Secret

Some pastoral situations are easier calls. If the allegations are about to surface in the media, an immediate public statement by the diocese is warranted. This would be the situation if the allegations were soon to be a matter of public record in the legal system. This would also be true if a victim were planning to release a statement to the press. If the allegations will inevitably reach the public forum, it is better that the diocese make the first announcement.

It would also be a simpler decision for the diocese if victims' families or victims who are now adults are adamant about wanting the situation to remain confidential or if the allegations of sexual misconduct appear to be highly dubious. Unless civil reporting requirements dictate otherwise, it would seem appropriate for the diocese to handle these cases discreetly.

The tough call is when a victim either does not object to the allegations becoming public or desires that the diocese make a public revelation. If the allegations of sexual abuse appear to have some merit, the diocese is caught between competing rights. Should an announcement be made or not?

There is no obvious answer. Victims' groups lobby for public announcement. Church officials often believe that maintaining confidentiality is the greater good. Each situation calls for a prudent pastoral judgment.

However, instead of all the burden, and the possible public blame, falling only on the shoulders of the bishop, I recommend that a team of professionals review each situation and present a recommendation to the ordinary. This group might be the same team of lay professionals that most dioceses have constituted as a review board on clerical sexual misconduct cases.

If the review board recommends that a case be dealt with discreetly, this would make the bishop less open to public criticism if the case eventually becomes known. It would also take some of the increasingly ponderous burden of clerical sexual misconduct cases off his shoulders.

In making a decision regarding public announcements, I offer the following guidelines for making such a judgment:

Err on the Side of the Victims. If the decision comes down to protecting victims or protecting the accused, and the allegations appear to have substance, we should err on the side of the victims. In each situation there will be competing rights. However, I believe the Church has a special responsibility to come to the aid of victims.

Better to Hear Bad News from the Church. When the parents of a family have bad news, such as an impending divorce, it is better for the children to hear the news from their parents than to learn it on the streets. In a similar way, it is better for the parishioners to hear about allegations of clerical sexual misconduct from Church officials than to read about such allegations in the newspaper.

Both of these guidelines suggest that the Church tell the truth to the parishioners. It is worth repeating the words of the November 1992 resolution of the American bishops: "Within the confines of respect for the privacy of the individuals involved, deal as openly as possible with members of the community."

I think it would be an exceptional case if secrecy were the best course of action, particularly if the allegations were substantiated. However, if the allegations remained questionable and the alleged victim asked for anonymity, a prudent silence might be most appropriate.

Signs of Progress

An increasing number of bishops are recognizing and responding to the trauma of parishes after allegations of clergy sexual misconduct. One of the first was Bishop Harry Flynn, formerly from the Diocese of Lafayette, Louisiana.

In 1984, when Father Gilbert Gauthe became the first priest in the United States to receive national public exposure as a child molester, the Diocese of Lafayette was assaulted with months of devastating national media attention. The media explored the details of Father Gauthe's behavior, revealed the names of other suspected priest-perpetrators, and charged the Church with a cover-up. The diocese lost millions of dollars in lawsuits. Parishioners were devastated. Eventually, Bishop Flynn was sent to Lafayette.

Bishop Flynn made it a personal priority to deal with the trauma that clergy involvement in sexual misconduct caused to the diocese. He met personally with victims. He visited affected parishes. He offered Mass and spoke to parishioners directly about the problem. He publicly announced his willingness to meet with anyone who had been victimized and encouraged victims of clergy misconduct to come forward. He offered an annual Mass in the cathedral for all victims of violence and abuse.

Bishop Flynn has the added gift of being able to understand the anger of victims and the people. He was able to listen compassionately and not become defensive as they vented their anger at the Church. Throughout the exchange, Bishop Flynn maintained a steady pastoral response of care and concern. He was a healing presence.

The Catholic Church in the United States is coming to realize that a priest who sexually molests children has a mental illness. He needs to confront his illness and accept assistance; his goal is to find recovery. We recognize that victims of sexual abuse must learn to face and overcome their trauma; their goal is to move from being victims to becoming survivors. The Church is starting to offer them support. But the parish community is also a victim. By confronting the problem openly and directly, with assistance from the bishop and his staff, it too can become a survivor.

These goals are not beyond reach. The pastoral and professional skills are available. Stories like those of Bishop Flynn and the Diocese of Lafayette have shown us what can be done. What remains for us is to recognize the wider trauma of clergy sexual misconduct and to mobilize our resources.

Clergy involvement in child sexual abuse has been a source of declining confidence in the Church. It need not be so. If we are able to maintain a steady pastoral response of care and concern while we face this tragedy directly, we can affirm the age-old confidence that people have had in the presence of Christ in the Catholic Church.

Chapter Four

Red Flags for
Child Sexual Abuse

No Silver Bullet

There is one thing that laity and Church officials agree upon: they are upset about children being sexually abused by Church ministers and they want it stopped. Parishioners and Church leaders alike have been devastated by the news of the sexual abuse of children by clergy. Thousands of children's lives have been marred. The credibility of the Church and its leadership has been hurt.

Both parents and Church leaders ask, "Is there not some way to identify pedophilic adults *before* they abuse our children?" Church officials have earnestly sought a "silver-bullet" that would take care of this problem once and for all. They have besought mental health professionals for a foolproof psychological screen to weed out potential molesters.

In response, one religious order's committee on sexual abuse suggested the use of polygraph tests and penile plethysmographies for every male candidate for their religious life. If implemented, an aspirant to a religious order would be asked a series of questions about sexual orientation and about past sexual behavior while connected to a lie detector.

Portions of this chapter were excerpted from an article by Stephen J. Rossetti, "Some Red Flags for Child Sexual Abuse," *Human Development* 15(4) (Winter 1994) 5–11.

Second, aspirants would be given a penile plethysmography. Such tests measure penile tumescence while the person is being shown sexually provocative slides of both genders and persons of varying ages. This assessment instrument is a biological way of measuring the strength of subjects' sexual attraction to female and male adults, adolescents, and children.

Indeed, polygraph tests and plethysmographies are sometimes used in assessments of persons charged with sexual, criminal offenses. But to use them on every person desirous of following a religious vocation or ministering in our churches is clearly unethical from a psychological perspective as well as being pastorally imprudent and insensitive. I suspect such use is illegal as well. These tests are highly invasive of one's privacy and are arguably not justified for widespread screening purposes.

There has been a search for less invasive testing of sexual arousal to minors. Other screening procedures similar to the plethysmography, such as the Abel Screen, are becoming available. However, the use of these tests for the widespread screening of candidates poses many of the same ethical problems cited above. They are too invasive of one's privacy to be used in general screening and the scientific validity of some of these tests remains to be firmly established.

Currently, there is no assessment tool available that is scientifically sound enough and sufficiently respective of one's privacy to be used as a general candidate screening tool for potential child sexual abusers. It is unlikely that such tools will be available for a long time. There is no silver bullet.

An Impenetrable Denial

Screening for sexual attraction to minors, both for pedophilia (attraction to prepubescent minors) and ephebophilia (attraction to postpubescent minors) is difficult, even for experienced psychologists who work regularly with sex offenders. Most often, adults afflicted with deviant sexual interests are largely indistinguishable from their peers . . . at least on the surface.

When interviewing adults with a sexual attraction to minors, they look "normal." They are often well-groomed and report few, if any, distressing symptoms. They are usually not excessively depressed or anxious. When given standard, objective measures of pathology, such as the Minnesota Multiphasic Personality Inventory (MMPI-2), the resulting profiles are largely within the normal ranges.

Using objective personality inventories, child sexual molesters look and test fine. It is little wonder that standard psychological screens previously used by Church organizations did not indicate a problem in men who ultimately would become molesters of children.

Coupled with this normal, undistressed presentation is often a sophisticated and sometimes impenetrable denial. When asked their sexual orientation, many perpetrators will say they are attracted to adult women. A few will claim to be attracted to adult men. It is rare for anyone to admit being sexually aroused by children.

Men charged with child sexual abuse often enter my office accompanied by a long list of alleged offenses. Nevertheless, they will protest their innocence. I ask, "Then how do you explain the fact that several children, none of whom know each other, have come forward accusing you of sexual molestation?" The usual response is: "I don't know" or they will concoct an implausible motivation attacking the credibility of the alleged victims, e.g., "These children are unbalanced" or "They misinterpreted my actions."

Even with written allegations in hand, screening of potential child molesters is difficult. But, without any clues of a sexual problem, screening adults for sexual attraction to minors can seem like groping in the dark. They will look fine. They will say they are fine. And objective personality measures will "confirm" that they are fine. But some of them will *not* be fine.

Something more needs to be done.

An Intensive Psychosexual History

While the denial of perpetrators is rarely penetrated by *objective* instruments, *projective* tests have been more successful. It is difficult for defensive evaluees to discern the "right" response to a Rorschach inkblot or to a Thematic Apperception Test (TAT) card. These and other projectives, such as Incomplete Sentences Blank and the House-Tree-Person Drawing Test, can sometimes suggest the presence of serious pathology despite the alleged perpetrators' best attempts at concealment. In particular, I have found the Exner Comprehensive Scoring System of the Rorschach to be especially able to divulge significant cognitive and emotional dysfunctions even though the objective personality screens revealed none.

But what I have found most essential in clinical assessments of candidates for ministry and of adults charged with child sexual abuse is an intensive, psychosexual history. While adult perpetrators of child sexual abuse rarely admit to others, or to themselves, a sexual attraction to minors, they often reveal similar patterns of psychosexual problems. By conducting an in-depth history and looking for psychosexual "red flags," a clinician can identify a significant percentage of adults who are at risk for sexually molesting minors.

It is important to note that this, too, is not a silver bullet. There will never be one instrument that can ferret out all those adults who might sexually molest children in the future. *This is due to the fact that child sexual abuse is a behavior and not a single diagnosis.* There are as many different clinical profiles of child sexual abusers as there are adults who abuse children.

For example, there are adults who are fixated pedophiles, i.e., sexually attracted to prepubescent children. There are others who are ephebophiles, i.e., sexually attracted to postpubescent children. Some have become psychosexually stuck in childhood. Others are reenacting childhood sexual traumas that they experienced. Some are violent: they might rape or kill their victims. Many more are passive and truly believe that they have been seduced by a sexually "precocious" child. The myriad of adults who sexually abuse children are clinically different.

Nevertheless, after interviewing and testing scores of adult ministers who sexually molest children, there are some commonalities which have surfaced. When trying to assess the possibility that an adult might be at risk for sexually molesting children in the future, or perhaps to determine the likelihood that current allegations of child sexual abuse against a person are true, the presence or absence of these psychosexual commonalities or red flags is an important clue.

Six Psychological Red Flags

1. *Confusion about Sexual Orientation.* By the time adults reach their mid-twenties, they should have an awareness and acceptance of their sexual orientation. Because of internal and external negative valuations of homosexuality, people who are sexually attracted to same-sex adults may take a few years longer. But the twenty-five- or thirty-five-year-old adult who cannot honestly admit his or her sexual orientation in the privacy of a clinical interview may be headed for trouble.

Being unaware of one's sexual orientation can occur for several reasons. Extremely naive or sheltered young adults may not know their sexual orientation. Adults suffering from long-standing major mental illnesses may never have been able to inquire about their sexuality. Young people who were given the message that sexual feelings are wrong likewise may not have become aware of their own sexual feelings. Many times people do not become fully aware of their sexual orientation because their sexual attractions would be a source of profound shame.

People who are sexually attracted to minors are often ashamed and disgusted by their own feelings. It is difficult enough to come to grips with a "normal" sexual orientation. But to face directly the fact that one is sexually aroused by minors is an awful task. It is psychically convenient for them to repress their sexual feelings altogether.

Adults sexually attracted to minors may become confused or unclear about their sexual orientation. During the psychosexual interview, when asked about their sexual orientation, their answers may be confusing, vague, or lacking in conviction. Further probing is needed.

Other times, adults attracted to children will say they are heterosexual or homosexual. This may be true. Many times adults who are sexually aroused by minors may also be aroused by adults as well. Thus, the fact that an alleged perpetrator of child sexual abuse has had successful sexual contact with another adult in the past does not preclude the possibility that the allegations are founded. Sometimes, however, their professed sexual attraction to adults is their wish and not reality. And they might have convinced themselves and really believe that they are not pedophilic or ephebophilic.

So, after asking someone's sexual orientation, the next question is crucial: "How do you know that this is your orientation?" If the declared heterosexual or homosexual orientation is only a wish, he or she will have difficulty explaining how they know what their orientation is. They may use platitudes such as: "I find adults attractive" or unconvincing statements such as: "I know I am heterosexual."

If the person claims to be heterosexual but has no sexual experience with women, I might ask if they have ever kissed a woman. Many young men, regardless of their sexual orientation, will have kissed a young woman in high school. If they say, "Yes," I will ask what the experience was like. One priest-perpetrator described it as a rather bland experience and then immediately spoke of his experiencing a call to celibate priesthood.

A major clue to their true orientation is found in their fantasy life. The consistent sexual objects of dreams or the sexual objects of masturbation fantasies are significant signs of their true orientation. For example, I remember a man who said he fantasized about rubbing suntan lotion on a woman's body by the pool; he found it a sexually pleasurable thought. His sensual description convinced me that he was truly heterosexually oriented.

If there is concern about candidates' awareness and acceptance of their sexual orientations, clinicians should probe further. While confusion about one's sexual orientation does not necessarily mean the hidden presence of a deviant pattern of sexual arousal, it clearly points out a major area for future personal growth.

I do not think that a person unaware of, or largely unaccepting of, his or her sexual orientation should be admitted into the major seminary or into the final years of religious formation. A time away from formation for personal inquiry into sexual questions is needed. *Major theology is not the time for candidates to be struggling with questions of sexual orientation.*

Confusion about sexual orientation is a red flag. Of itself, this confusion may not be indicative that the person has a hidden sexual attraction to minors. It could be the result of a variety of sexual conflicts or simply the result of a slowed psychosexual development.

There are other red flags that are likely to be present in the history of an ephebophile or pedophile.

2. *Childish Interests and Behavior.* Adults who sexually molest children often suffer from gross emotional immaturity. For instance, one woman, mother of four and married to a pedophile, complained that she had to take care of five children. Her husband acted like a child and related to his wife as a mother.

While pedophiles and ephebophiles may have the body of a thirty-, forty- or fifty-year-old, their psychic age is closer to that of a child. It is not surprising, therefore, that they act like children and have childish interests.

Sometimes it is helpful to ask adults accused of child molestation about their hobbies or what movies they have recently enjoyed. One pedophile said he delighted in playing Santa Claus for the children. Another spoke of building train sets and taking children to amusement parks. A third mentioned three different movies he liked the most: all were children's stories. A childish person will have childish interests. Other adults will often perceive them as childlike or naive.

Often, real children will gravitate to them. These immature adults understand children and can emotionally connect with them. Finding an adult that has the same immature psychic organization as they can be a powerful attraction for children. It is little wonder that such adults become "pied pipers" and are known as effective with children. The truth is: *they are children themselves.*

It may be difficult to distinguish between the person who has a special gift of working with children and the childish adult who is sexually aroused by children. Externally, both may look the same, i.e., they have an effective way of attracting and speaking to children and are often found with children around them.

A discerning question to ask is: With whom do you spend your time off and vacations? Pedophiles or ephebophiles are more likely to spend their free time with minors. Healthy adults will spend their free time with other adults. We vacation and recreate with those we feel most comfortable; we spend our free time with those who are most like ourselves.

One of the largest red flags for pedophilia is an adult who vacations and spends free time with other people's children.

3. *Lack of Peer Relationships.* The other side of the coin to the previous red flag, "childish interests and behaviors," is a "lack of

peer relationships." Child molesters often recreate with children and they rarely, if ever, have satisfying relationships with other adults. As psychic children, they do not have the emotional tools to connect with their peers.

Put a pedophile in a parish and he will eventually be spending his energy working with the children. His relationships with adults will likely be superficial and/or stereotypical. Child molesters very often feel inadequate around other adults. They feel like children and do not feel competent around people their own age.

During psychological assessments, I will ask them who is their closest friend. Not uncommonly, they will mention a minor. Similarly, I may ask what personal relationships have been most meaningful for them. Again, some will speak of their relationships with minors.

Having a lack of peer relationships may not always be easy to discern. First, if the molester is a priest, he may engage in stereotyped priest-parishioner relationships with relative ease. He may be externally friendly and pastorally caring. Since the majority of parishioners relate to their priests in these stereotypical ways, most of the people will view this priest as being nice, although perhaps a bit distant. Few will realize that he does not have satisfying personal relations with peers.

Second, it is difficult to discern if a perpetrator does not have intimate relations because many of them will believe and attempt to portray their peer relations as being close ones. It is common that child molesters will not know what an intimate relationship is like since many of them have never experienced one. Thus, they will declare that their peer relationships are deep and intimate.

However, further probing will reveal little sharing of life and support with "friends." The following questions might be helpful: "How often do you see your best friend?" "What do you do together?" "What do you talk about?" "How do you know when you need emotional support and where do you go to get it?" "How much of yourself do you reveal to your friends?" This probing will probably reveal that the pedophile's "close" adult friends are merely acquaintances.

I believe that *the strongest sign of psychological health is the existence of intimate and satisfying peer relationships.* A lack of peer relationships in an adult is clearly a red flag. Some of these adults without peer relationships will be at risk for sexually abusing children. The majority are likely to have serious psychological impairments. I cannot imagine such a person being a suitable candidate for ministry.

4. *Extremes in Developmental Sexual Experiences.* When conducting a psychosexual history, evaluees should be asked directly and explicitly about their sexual experiences throughout their lives. Did you experience any childhood sex play? Was there any sexual exploration? What was puberty like? Did you date? What sexual contacts have you had with people of the same sex and with the opposite sex?

I have found that adults who sexually abuse children often fall into one of two extremes: they either had an excessive amount of sexual stimulation as a child or they can recount almost no sexual experience whatever.

There is a common series of sexual experiences in many healthy adults' developments. It is normal that children would have one or two experiences of "playing doctor" or looking and touching the sexual parts of other children of approximately the same age. Puberty is likely to have been an unsettling time for most children but they manage to get through it. Masturbation as an adolescent is common. Normal adolescents will begin exploring their sexuality with their peers through dating, kissing, fondling, and other kinds of sexual encounters.

Some pedophiles or ephebophiles will report unusual amounts of sexual contact as a child. There may be numerous instances of childhood sex play. In early adolescence, some become involved in group masturbation circles and/or extensive sexual contact with a cousin or a neighborhood youth. Extensive sexual contact with siblings is possible.

Some adult perpetrators have reported compulsive masturbation as a teenager: up to several times a day. Others have a long history of mutual masturbation with their peers. A few have reported extended incestuous relationships with brothers, sisters, or cousins. Some have recounted excessive sexual stimulation from their earliest years.

Such people are sexually overstimulated as children. It is possible that they become psychosexually "stuck" as children. Many of them learned that the way to relate to others, especially to other children, is with sex. As adults, they have continued relating to young children as sexual objects.

On the other extreme are those who report a lack of any sexual contact whatever. They may never have masturbated or began masturbating late, e.g., in their twenties. They report no history of childhood sex play. Some deny dating or engaging in adolescent sexual exploration.

When asked about their sexual fantasies, they will say they have none. Sexuality was not discussed in the family; it was a taboo subject. They may even have problems identifying someone that they currently find sexually attractive. In short, sexuality has been erased from their conscious life.

Conducting a sexual history with such people is unusually brief: nothing happened. In some cases, the person is simply lying. They are afraid to reveal their true experiences for fear of what will happen. Other times, however, there really has been no conscious experience of their sexuality.

There are people who have had no sexual experience and are still basically psychologically healthy. However, I suspect that it is more often the case that the person is ashamed of, frightened of, and/or has repressed any sexual urges, impulses, thoughts, or fantasies. Such people try to live as if they were not sexual beings. This will cause a variety of psychological symptoms. Eventually, such repressions are likely to fail, especially under stress.

I remember one pedophile who was so ashamed of his sexuality that he vowed to live "like an angel." He said he was "beyond" such things as sexual desires because of prayer and God's grace. He went on to say that he believed that a truly holy person would not have sexual struggles.

Eventually, this angel crashed. After twenty years of sexual repression, he went through a painful succession of personal losses. His ministry was particularly difficult and the normal struggles of midlife added to his overall level of stress. He became sexually active with a number of early adolescent males.

Adults who report sexual overstimulation as children or, conversely, who report little, if any, sexual awareness may be at risk for sexual problems in the future. Such extremes are a psychosexual red flag.

These adults may or may not be attracted to minors. Regardless, it is unlikely that they have a balanced and healthy integration of their sexuality.

5. *Personal History of Childhood Sexual Abuse and/or Deviant Sexual Experiences.* Another red flag in a psychosexual history is the presence of childhood sexual abuse and/or other deviant sexual experiences. Approximately two-thirds of the priests we have evaluated for the sexual molestation of minors have themselves been sexually molested as children.

It must be said that the large majority of people who are sexually molested as children do NOT go on to abuse other children. I have heard of dioceses that will not accept candidates who admit that they have been sexually molested. This is unfortunate. Many people who experience childhood sexual molestation go on to live happy, productive lives. Nevertheless, childhood sexual abuse is a risk factor for future perpetration.

However, simply asking a subject about a history of sexual abuse may not yield the truth. Many times perpetrators do not recognize true instances of their own abuse.

For example, one man had been fondled repeatedly by a cousin who was six years older. He said it was not sexual abuse because he found pleasure in the experience. However, upon deeper inquiry, he revealed that the encounters made him increasingly embarrassed. He felt manipulated and used. He could not extricate himself from the relationship and the contacts ended only after the cousin moved away.

If the person being evaluated does not report any history of sexual abuse, I would follow up with a question such as: "Did you ever experience someone older than you looking or touching you in a way that was sexual? If so, what happened?" Unrecognized sexual abuse is common and suggests that the abuse experienced remains unprocessed and unhealed.

But not all perpetrators have been sexually molested as children. Many of them have experienced other types of deviant childhood sexual experiences. Perhaps a parent will be raped in front of the children. Sexual boundaries in the family may be excessively loose such as parents bathing or dressing in front of children or lounging around the house with their sexual parts exposed. A few will report an unusual encounter with a peer such as prepubescent oral sex.

In their later years, some perpetrators will frequent pornographic shops and consistently use lewd magazines and videos. Others will cruise for sexual partners and engage in anonymous sex. Some will have a long history of brief sexual encounters. A few will reveal that they sexually stimulated a young child when they were in late adolescence.

Obviously, evaluees will be hesitant to admit such deviant sexual experiences. However, during a clinical psychosexual interview, such questions should be asked directly, e.g., "Have you ever had a sexual encounter with someone you did not know before that day?" "Have you ever used 'adult' magazines or videos, or magazines or videos with pictures of children, or magazines or videos that others might consider to be pornographic?"

Adults with deviant sexual interests usually will try to hide the truth of these experiences during a clinical interview. If a general question is asked about deviant sexual experiences, the answer is likely to come back in the negative. The interviewer is much more likely to receive a truthful answer if specific questions are posed, e.g., "Did you ever pay someone to have sex?"

The presence of deviant sexual experiences, including sexual abuse, are significant red flags in a psychosexual history. It is true that some candidates will simply lie about previous sexual experiences. However, many will not. And experienced clinicians can sometimes sense when the evaluee is not being truthful.

The presence of some types of deviant sexual experiences should be immediate grounds for rejection as ministerial candidates. For example, I cannot think of any reason to accept a candidate who had sexually molested young children when he or she was in adolescence. Other experiences should be explored and the amount of subsequent healing should be considered.

Many victims of sexual abuse have made fine ministers. But the wounds incurred by the abuse should have been addressed and opened to God's healing before acceptance.

6. *An Excessively Passive, Dependent, Conforming Personality.* While conducting a psychosexual history, the interviewer will develop a sense of the evaluee's personality style. When coupled

with the results of personality inventories, such as the Millon Clinical Multiaxial Inventory, Third Edition (MCMI–III) and the evaluee's own statements about self, a coherent picture of the subject's personality should emerge. I have found child molesters with many different traits such as narcissistic, asocial, and/or histrionic personalities. But there is one common type of child molester in ministry whose personality is passive, dependent, and conforming.

A little dependency and a conforming attitude is not a bad feature for someone in ministry. Parishioners like a minister who does not come on too strong and who is anxious to please. Formation programs tend to reward those who obey the rules and do not make waves. People want their ministers to be nice.

However, a number of the male ministers who sexually abuse children will have a personality disorder whose predominant traits include passivity, dependency, and compulsivity.

This type of child molester will almost always elevate the "Dependent" and "Compulsive" scales on the Millon Clinical Multiaxial Inventory (MCMI–III). However, such elevations should be viewed with caution because many adults who fit in well in large institutions will exhibit such personality traits. What will be striking is how passive and conforming these persons come across in the course of the psychological interview.

For example, some will describe their participation in relationships in overly passive ways. They may complain of being used and manipulated by other people. Some will see themselves continually in a victim stance. Most will try their best to smile at others and to please. During the clinical interview, one of their major goals will be to please the interviewer.

When dealing with authority, these people are overly respectful and deferential. At times, they can become perfectionistic. It will be important for them to be seen in a good light by others, especially by their superiors. They want to be good and they want to be liked.

Unfortunately, this personality style usually hides a deep sense of personal insecurity. Their self-esteem is low. They often harbor a buried resentment toward others and toward authority figures. Since it is important for these people to be liked, they usually bury their true feelings, wants, and desires. They do their best to bury their anger, too. They often describe themselves as "quiet and fearful" people.

In ministerial situations, such people often spiritually rationalize their lack of healthy assertiveness by speaking of holy obedience and doing the will of others. While Christian spirituality has a proper place of esteem for true obedience and self-denial, these dependent-compulsive people do not find freedom in their excessive acts of self-denial. They are slaves to their own fears.

This personality style is a complement to the earlier red flags of poor peer relationships and childish behavior. When people feel inadequate with other adults, they may try to hide their inadequacies behind an agreeable and pliable exterior. Since many of them do not feel they can express their true selves, they try to be what others want them to be.

This personality disorder does not allow the person to receive the human connection and warmth that is so necessary for a healthy life. When this personality organization breaks down, and it usually does, it can manifest itself in a variety of ways. One of the ways is sexual. For those who find minors sexually available and attractive, the chance of a sexual offense is significant.

While there are a variety of personality styles associated with adults who sexually abuse minors, there is one type that seems to be common among male perpetrators in ministry. During the course of the psychosexual interview, the clinician should be alert to the signs that the subject is excessively passive, dependent, and conforming. This is the last red flag.

Training and Education Needed

Any red flag found by itself does not necessarily mean that the subject will be sexually interested in minors. For example, there are many shy, introverted people who do not have good peer relations; this does not mean they are pedophiles. There are many people who are childlike and naive; they, too, are not necessarily sexually interested in children.

Nevertheless, when an evaluee shows a number of these psychological red flags, serious concerns should be raised. Even if there is not a pedophilic or ephebophilic sexual orientation, the presence of these red flags suggests the need for intensive psychotherapeutic work.

Candidates who believe that a commitment to a celibate lifestyle will help them put their sexual problems behind them are headed for trouble. How many perpetrators of child sexual abuse have told me that they thought that celibate ministry would take care of their sexual struggles! Many of them had no problems for the first ten or fifteen years of ministry. Eventually, an unresolved sexual problem will out.

No one argues that an in-depth psychosexual history is inappropriate for a clinical assessment of alleged sex offenders. In a confidential setting and when accomplished by a skilled clinician, a psychosexual history is an essential part of the assessment process.

Some have asked if it is not a violation of one's personal privacy to conduct an in-depth psychosexual history for all candidates for priesthood and the religious life. I would argue that the needs of the Church and the demands of ministry today necessitate this history-taking. In reality, today's generation is well accustomed to frankness in sexual matters.

Ideally, subjects will demonstrate a healthy, integrated sense of sexuality. During the course of the psychosexual interview, they should have an awareness of and comfort with their sexual orientations. In a confidential clinical interview, they should be able to speak about their sexuality in open and honest ways.

I doubt that there will ever be a "silver bullet" that will assuredly identify all potential child molesters. However, the mainstay of any assessment process in determining risk for sexual offense will be an intensive psychosexual interview.

The quality of the interview will directly reflect the experience and training of the clinician conducting the session. Most often, well-trained and experienced clinicians will be attuned to risk factors for child sexual abuse and spot them in the course of the interview. Clinicians without this background can listen to the same interview and miss its significance entirely.

Perhaps what is most indicated today is not a magic screen to solve all our problems. Rather, the order of the day suggests the need for education and training. Clinical personnel who assess alleged child abusers and screen candidates for ministry need to be trained in giving psychosexual histories. Clinical experts in this field need to share the fruits of their experience. Church and societal leaders need to facilitate this process.

Even with better education and training, we will not stop all child sexual abuse before it occurs. We can, however, expect to make substantial progress. Rather than waiting for a future development that is unlikely to occur, we can make much progress with what we have today. Now is the time to begin.

Chapter Five

Suicides of Priests and the Crisis of Faith

Clerical Suicides Increasing

On June 4, 1994, Fr. John Hesch of the Diocese of Richmond put a gun to his head and pulled the trigger. Several hours earlier, he had been confronted with allegations of child sexual abuse. Next to his body lay written notes claiming his innocence.

One year earlier, Fr. Thomas Smith of the Archdiocese of Baltimore put a twelve-gauge shotgun to his head and ended his life. Allegations that he had sexually abused a young boy were presented to him on August 19, 1993. Two days later, he was dead.

One year before Fr. Smith's death, the chancellor of the Diocese of Arlington, Msgr. William Reinecke, died at the Trappist abbey of Berryville, Virginia. After his death a young man came forward alleging that he had previously confronted Msgr. Reinecke with charges of sexual molestation. The Chancellor obliterated himself with a shotgun on August 11, 1992.

A priest from Alabama shot himself in 1986 after being accused of sexually molesting a twelve-year-old boy. The sixty-one-

Portions of this chapter originally appeared as: Stephen J. Rossetti, "Priest Suicides and The Crisis of Faith," *America,* 171(13) (October 29, 1994) 8–12, and as "The Mark of Cain: Reintegrating Pedophiles," *America,* 173(6) (September 9, 1995) 9–16.

year-old priest left a note saying that he would rather be "a dead memory than a living disgrace."[1]

These priests are not the only ones who have died at their own hands in the wake of allegations of child sexual abuse. There have been several others and the list is growing.

Despised by Society

In treatment, a most difficult clinical task for priest-perpetrators of child sexual abuse is breaking through the initial denial. Even in the face of overwhelming evidence, many of these men still have great difficulty admitting to others, and to themselves, that they are guilty.

If they do admit some guilt, it is usually minimized or rationalized to reduce the severity of their actions or to shift the blame from themselves to the victims. During clinical evaluations, I often hear statements like, "The boy was coming on to me" or "It wasn't sex, we were just horsing around." The perpetrator who can honestly admit the facts and accept responsibility is well on the road to recovery.

Defense mechanisms, including denial and minimization, have a positive function. They protect the human psyche from being given too much to handle at one time. When a priest is confronted with allegations of child sexual abuse, it is almost always a situation of psychic overload.

Up until the allegations surface, a priest is presented to the world as a man of God. He wants to think of himself as someone who is good and kind. He has no wife or children, few possessions, little money, and no home. Perhaps his only worldly possession is his good reputation and a position of honor among his parishioners. Allegations of sexual misconduct not only strip him of his reputation, society will instantly *despise* him.

Even in prison, the child molester is loathed and at risk of being harmed by other inmates. For their own safety, incarcerated priests are sometimes placed in confinement. One priest told me that the other inmates mocked him, abused him, and called out,

---

[1]S. Shane, "Priest's suicide reveals long history of abuse," *Baltimore Sun*, September 5, 1993, p. 22A.

"There goes that priest-diddler." Another said he was in solitary confinement for twenty-three out of twenty-four hours a day with one hour a day of supervised exercise.

Banished from Society

There are many who would banish child molesters from living among the populace altogether. A rapidly increasing number of states are requiring public notification of child molesters released from prison. For example, New York State passed a law to make information available on sex offenders through a 900 telephone number.[2] Similarly, California has set up a 900 number and, for four dollars, a person can inquire whether someone they know has been convicted of child sexual abuse. In Louisiana, child sexual abusers are required by law to send written notices to their neighbors about their presence.[3]

It is not surprising that these laws have spawned a number of violent acts. After "Megan's Law" was passed in New Jersey requiring public notification of sex offenders' addresses, a man who lived in the same residence as a sex offender was mistakenly beaten up. In the state of Washington, a rapist's future residence was burned down when the community became aware that he was soon to move in. It is not just the prison population that despises and beats up sex offenders.

In a new twist, several states have passed laws which allow state officials to continue confinement of sexual offenders beyond their prison terms. Mitchell Gaff was sent to a center for sexual predators in Washington State after serving a ten-year sentence in prison. Under its new "sexual predator" law, the prosecutors sought indefinite confinement for Gaff after his prison term ran out. The proceedings are akin to those used in civil courts to confine the insane. Similar statutes have been passed in Wisconsin, New Jersey, and Kansas.[4]

[2] R. Hanley, "New Jersey High Court Upholds Law Identifying Sex Offenders," *New York Times,* July 26, 1995, pp. 1, B2.
[3] B. Meier, "'Sexual Predators' Finding Sentence May Last Past Jail," *New York Times,* February 27, 1995, p. B8.
[4] Ibid., A1.

This extreme social reaction to child molesters is not confined to the United States. In Scotland, John Bancroft, M.D., wrote: "It is difficult to avoid the conclusion that in many cases the social reaction against the paedophile and the severity of the sentences imposed on him by the courts are out of proportion to the gravity of his offence."[5]

Clerical Prisons

Not surprisingly, the Catholic Church is under the same pressure as the secular society to name publicly and to ostracize priests known to have sexually molested minors. Thus, Catholic dioceses are becoming increasingly unwilling to take priest-offenders back into their ranks.

What happens to such clerics? If they refuse to request laicization, and many do refuse, the Church has nowhere to put them. In one diocese, the Church sought a change in zoning to establish a house for such unassignable priests. The response of the secular community was overwhelmingly negative. The diocese tried again in another location and was met with the same response. Eventually, they gave up.

In response to a mounting need, clerical "warehouses" are springing up. These are long-term care facilities, sometimes isolated from population centers, where these men reside. Warehouses offer a minimum of services and charge a modest daily fee to the sponsoring religious organization. At best, such places can be Christian communities of societal outcasts; at worst, they become clerical prisons.

Societal Lepers

One cannot help but recall the work of Fr. Damien and the lepers of Molokai. People with Hansen's disease did not request asylum. An 1865 law passed in Hawaii made it mandatory for victims of this disease to present themselves to the Board of Health.

---

[5]John Bancroft, *Human Sexuality and Its Problems,* 2nd ed. (New York: Church Livingstone, 1989) 697.

Some families would not hand over their sick members and tried to shelter them. The police were sent to hunt them down. Many lepers fled to the hills and to the caves. The police used bloodhounds to search them out.

The victims of Hansen's disease were sent to a settlement in Molokai by Hawaii's government officials who feared the contagion would spread. Their fear was a mixture of clinical facts and centuries of misinformation that fueled an irrational response to the disease. False legends and popular myths made those afflicted with Hansen's disease a dreaded people.

It might be argued that child molesters are different from those with Hansen's disease in that they are guilty of a *crime* while lepers suffer from a *physical* disease. It is true that child molesters have committed a crime against our most vulnerable young people.

Indeed, I believe that those who commit any crime, including that of child sexual abuse, should be subjected to the criminal justice system for the sake of society and for their own sakes. More than one priest-offender has told me that he was glad that he served time in prison for his offenses. He said he needed to repay a debt to society.

But, like leprosy, those who sexually molest children almost always suffer from some sort of psychological disorder which spawns their aberrant behavior. *Pedophilia is an illness.* Just as serious as physical illnesses, mental illnesses should be diagnosed and treated with the best available clinical procedures.

What is striking is the volatility of society's response to the child molester and the vengeance with which he is faced. There are many other heinous crimes which do not engender the same response. There are no similar movements afoot to identify and restrict serial killers, drug dealers, child-beaters, cop-killers, and psychopaths. Child sex molesters are singled out for particular loathing and punishment which is now being institutionalized by state governments. Truly, they have become leprous societal outcasts.

Hysteria Fueled by Myth

Just as the banishment of lepers was fueled by medieval myths, the hysteria surrounding the perpetrators of child sexual abuse is exacerbated by myths about those who suffer from sexual deviancies. Child molesters incarnate our deepest childhood fears: we imagine them to be old, evil and malicious men. In our minds' eye, we see them as powerful and dark figures that lurk in the shadows and prey on the unsuspecting.

The media used words like "monster" to describe priest-child molester James Porter. One expected him to appear as a voracious, menacing figure who would strike terror in people's hearts. What appeared on television was a weak, frightened, confused, and ineffectual man.

Our myths about child molesters come more from the projections of what lies within our own inner psyches than from the truth about who these men are. In fact, they are often ineffectual men whose dysfunctional upbringing did not afford them the chance to learn and to act like competent, empowered adults.

We are aghast when a priest, accused of child sexual abuse, ends his life and wonder how he could do it. Considering the above, I am surprised that more do not. It is difficult to remain in this world as a leprous outcast or as a "living disgrace."

Facing the Truth

In the survey I conducted of 1,810 active Catholics in the United States and Canada, the respondents were presented with the statement: "I expect a priest's moral conduct to be better than other people's conduct." Table 1 compares the percentage of agreement by the laity in the sample with the percentage by priests. The results were illuminating.

Table 1	
Priest's Moral Conduct Should Be Better	
*Percent (%) **Agreement***	
80.9	87.5
Active Lay Catholics	Priests
Sample N = 1,013	Sample N = 314

Despite our conscious awareness that priests, like all of us, are flawed human beings, the large majority of active Catholics in North America still expect their priests to act better than the laity.

The presbyterate shares their belief. Priests expect their own conduct to be better than the laity's conduct. In fact, priests are even more likely to set a higher standard for themselves. If the laity are demanding of our priests, priests are even tougher on themselves.

It is difficult to accept the fact of anyone sexually molesting a child. When a priest is the perpetrator, a symbol of the divine and a despicable act meet in dismaying juxtaposition. It is little wonder that the flood of clergy sexual misconduct cases into the public forum has been a shock. The above data suggest that the group most shocked by allegations of clergy-child sexual abuse is the clergy themselves.

I remember giving an all-day workshop a year ago on clergy-child sexual abuse to a group of clerics. After a six-hour presentation on the clinical roots of sexual abuse, one cleric stood up looking obviously upset. In a high-pitched, stressed voice, he said, "So these newspaper stories of abuse are true!?! I thought they were all made up." I had spent a day discussing some of the clinical nuances of clerical sexual abuse cases; he had spent the day struggling to accept the fact that they occurred at all.

Just as the defense mechanism of "denial" serves to protect the perpetrator from psychic overload, denial can also protect other clerics, and perhaps an entire community of faith, from facing fully and directly the terrible shock of clergy-child sexual abuse. But when the denial breaks down and the truth comes rushing in, there is a terrible time of struggle.

Our communities of faith are going through such a struggle. For example, even when overwhelming evidence exists that a priest is guilty of sexually abusing minors, and perhaps has been legally convicted of such crimes, more than a few will cling to a belief in the man's innocence. Some will find fault with the legal system. Others will blame the victims. Most will wonder, "How could this be true?"

Priest-perpetrators are individually entering the same struggle. "Shame" is too mild a word for the self-loathing they feel. One said he felt like "walking shame." Another called himself "scum." Do they have a right to live?

Perhaps the growing number of priest-suicides is a symptom of a society that is having difficulty coming to terms with the truth. It may be that the act of a priest obliterating his face with a shotgun is symbolic of the hatred we have expressed for the child molester. Many wish they would just disappear. An increasing number of priest-perpetrators agree.

Beyond Hope?

I do not blame the secular press. They have zealously exposed the evil that is child sexual abuse. If they did not, most of us would not know that many of our children are being sexually abused. We would still be living in a comfortable ignorance.

I do not blame our legal system. The monetary damages the Church has suffered, and continues to suffer, have forced us to address this issue.

Both the legal system and the secular press have done their duties. But the impressions they have given of the clinical status of perpetrators and victims are not always accurate.

At the 1994 National LINKUP Conference, an organization dedicated to serving victims of clerical sexual abuse, one of the main speakers was a legal advocate for victims. She said that civil proceedings can be difficult for victims of clerical sexual abuse. One major reason is that the victim's defense attorney will present the psychic wounds the victim has suffered in the strongest of terms. The description will make the wounds out to be lifelong and paralyzing. Listening to such court testimony, victims may end up feeling like permanently damaged goods.

Similarly, the media, in an attempt to portray the true evil that is child sexual abuse has, at times, unwittingly portrayed victims as hopelessly damaged. The media have come dangerously close to re-victimizing them.

In an inspiring address at the same LINKUP conference, one speaker warned victims against remaining stuck in their victimization. He outlined a path of recovery and encouraged LINKUP members to move from being victims to becoming survivors. He himself was a witness to the power of healing. As a child, he had been sexually molested by Reverend James Porter. After years of powerlessness and pain, he was now walking this path toward inner peace.

Just like victims of sexual abuse, there is healing for the perpetrators. They, too, can find the road to recovery. Unfortunately, many media reports suggest that perpetrators, too, are untreatable. They say, "Pedophilia is incurable." They give the impression that perpetrators are hopelessly damaged.

Successful Treatment vs. Cure

The statement, "Pedophilia is incurable," is misleading. First of all, most perpetrators of child sexual abuse are not pedophiles. In a Saint Luke Institute sample of 280 priests who had sexually molested minors, only 20 percent were actually pedophiles. Pedophilia is a clinical term referring to someone whose sexual orientation is towards a prepubescent child. It is true that psychotherapy usually cannot change one's sexual orientation. The minority of perpetrators of child sexual abuse are actually diagnosable pedophiles. Their treatment focuses on helping them control their deviant sexual desires. Even with this significantly impaired group, there have been many successful treatment cases.

The majority of perpetrators are involved with postpubescent children. All things being equal, they are more amenable to treatment. One of their goals is to develop satisfying relationships with age-appropriate peers. They are assisted in the healing of their own childhood wounds and in growing into an emotional and sexual adulthood. Prior to treatment, many of them are psychosexually "stuck" in early adolescence.

Modern psychology shuns the word "cure" for any mental condition whether it is depression, anxiety, schizophrenia or pedophilia. However, it does speak of "successful treatment." Can perpetrators of child sexual abuse be successfully treated? The answer is clearly, "Yes." The development of new therapeutic techniques and advances in psychopharmacology have dramatically increased our successes.

Recidivism Rates

There is some basis in fact for this past pessimism regarding the "incurable" nature of child molesters. Marshall et al. noted that "recidivism data up to the late 1960s are certainly not encouraging."[6] The earliest treatment modalities often employed individual, insight-oriented psychotherapy. Just as this regimen has proven largely ineffective in treating alcoholics in the midst of their addiction, it has not been effective with child molesters. The perpetrators' denial, lack of motivation, and tendencies to minimize their actions make them unsuitable candidates for such therapies.[7] In addition, many early studies relied upon a highly impaired and compulsive group of incarcerated subjects who were more likely to re-offend.

Newer treatment modalities have become available in the last twenty years which have substantially increased the likelihood of successful treatment. A review of the literature by Marshall et al. concluded that comprehensive cognitive/behavioral programs and anti-androgens medications (e.g., Depo-Provera) were "unequivocally positive" in treating child molesters. However, they cautioned that "not all programs are successful and not all sex offenders profit from treatment."[8]

Like the Marshall et al. findings, Saint Luke Institute, a program that specializes in the treatment of priest-perpetrators, has found that low doses, e.g., 250 mg/weekly, of Depo-Provera significantly lower the serum testosterone level in males, and thus reduce the intensity of sexual urges, while having a minimum of side effects. This form of "chemical castration" is reversible. It is used as a temporary means of reducing sexual drives in order to allow patients a period of calm in which to explore their sexuality and to implement more functional strategies in its management.

Fred Berlin, M.D., conducted a study of 173 treatment-compliant pedophiles and 126 treatment-*non*compliant pedophiles at the Johns Hopkins Sexual Disorders Clinic. Five to six years after treatment began, the recidivism rate was 11.1 percent for the treatment-noncompliant group and only 2.9 percent for the treatment-compliant group.[9] Most of the noncompliant group

[6]W. L. Marshall, R. Jones, T. Ward, P. Johnson, and H. E. Barbaree, "Treatment Outcome with Sex Offenders," *Clinical Psychology Review* 11 (1991) 474.

[7]L. S. Grossman, "Research Directions in the Evaluation and Treatment of Sex Offenders: An Analysis," *Behavioral Sciences and the Law* 3(4) (1985) 424.

[8]Marshall et al., "Treatment Outcome with Sex Offenders," 480.

[9]F. S. Berlin, W. P. Hunt, H. M. Malin, A. Dyer, G. K. Lehne, and S. Dean, "A Five-Year Plus Follow-Up Survey of Criminal Recidivism Within a Treated

had received a significant amount of therapy but had ultimately been discharged for failure to attend sessions. Similarly, a Canadian study of 33 pedophiles used a sexual addictions model in treatment and had only a 3 percent recidivist rate over a five-year period.[10]

In the ten years in which Saint Luke Institute has treated over three hundred Catholic priests who have sexually molested minors, they currently know of only two who have relapsed into child sexual abuse. While it is likely that there are others whom they do not know about, their experience to date suggests that it is improbable that a priest will relapse if he has done well in residential treatment, complied with their five-year aftercare program, and has engaged in ongoing supervision and outpatient treatment.

It should be noted that published data on recidivism rates are not uniformly positive. Furby et al. found a wide range of recidivism rates across many clinical studies.[11] While there are reasons to be optimistic about the results of newer treatments, some caution and a healthy skepticism are not unwarranted.

Priest-Perpetrators Are Often Treatable

Adele Mayer listed a number of negative treatment indicators for sex-offenders including: evidence of violent behavior, low IQ/capacity for insight, sexual abuse of very young children, organic brain deficits, and severe character disorder.[12] The clinical experience at Saint Luke Institute supports Mayer's findings. Perpetrators with serious neuropsychological deficits, offenses against younger prepubescent minors, serious personality disorders, a rigid denial and/or a long history of compulsive abuse of many children are poor treatment risks.

Cohort of 406 Pedophiles, 111 Exhibitionists and 109 Sexual Aggressives: Issues and Outcome," *American Journal of Forensic Psychiatry* 12(3) (1991) 17–18.

[10]K. R. Graham, "The Sexual Addiction Model in Treatment of Incarcerated Offenders: A Study on Recidivism," *Sexual Addiction and Compulsivity: The Journal of Treatment and Prevention* 1(3) (1994) 278–283.

[11]L. Furby, M. R. Weinrott, and L. Blackshaw, "Sex Offender Recidivism: A Review," *Psychological Bulletin* 105(1) (1989) 27.

[12]A. Mayer, *Sex Offenders: Approaches To Understanding and Management* (Holmes Beach, Fla.: Adele Mayer Learning Publications, Inc., 1988) 44–45.

Fortunately, most of the priests who offend against minors do NOT have these negative treatment indicators. For example, the landmark study by Abel et al. found that 377 non-incarcerated child molesters, who victimized children outside the home, had an average of 72.72 victims and an average of 128.11 total acts of abuse.[13] On the other hand, in a Saint Luke Institute sample of 84 priest-child molesters, the average number of victims was 8.52 and the average number of total sexual contacts with minors was 32.14. The latter data suggest that priest-perpetrators of child sexual abuse are likely to commit fewer acts against fewer victims.

In fact, priest-offenders have tended to be intelligent, adequately functioning men, many of whom otherwise had good ministries. For example, in a sample of 224 priest-child molesters at Saint Luke Institute, the average IQ score was 122. This places them in the upper 7 percent of the general population. It would be statistically misleading to compare the likelihood of treatment success on these higher-functioning priests using modern treatment modalities with outdated methods used on incarcerated, lower-functioning patients.

Similarly, Fred Berlin, M.D., noted that "media can distort public perceptions of treatment outcome" for sex offenders and such distortions have aided in "creating a climate of opinion that is unjustifiably biased against psychiatric care."[14]

Will People Take Them Back?

But even if further clinical studies show that some priest-perpetrators are at minimal risk for re-offending, societal stereotypes and myths will remain. Will church members be willing to reintegrate some of them back into ministry?

The 1,810 active Roman Catholics from the United States and Canada that I surveyed were presented the statement: "A priest

[13]G. Abel, J. Becker, M. Mittelman, J. Cunningham-Rathner, J. Rouleau, and W. Murphy, "Self-Reported Sex Crimes of Nonincarcerated Paraphiliacs," *Journal of Interpersonal Violence* 2 (1987) 19.

[14]F. S. Berlin and H. M. Malin, "Media Distortion of the Public's Perception of Recidivism and Psychiatric Rehabilitation," *American Journal of Psychiatry* 148(11) (November 1991) 1573.

who abuses children should *not* be allowed to return to ministry." The responses were as follows:

Table 2
"A priest who abuses children should *not*
be allowed to return to ministry."

Percent (%) Agreement

42	31	27
% agreement	% unsure	% disagreement

(sample N = 1,810)

The survey results indicated that active Catholics were divided on the issue. There were a solid number of people who opposed returning priests-offenders to ministry. Of the 42 percent who opposed their return, more than half of them indicated they felt *strongly* that child molesters should not be returned. Any bishop or superior who returns a priest-offender to ministry will have to bear in mind that there will be a significant number of people who will not agree with his decision.

But there were many unanswered questions inherent in this survey question such as: "What sort of ministry would he be returning to?" and "Under what conditions?" In the same survey, I therefore asked them to respond to a second statement: "I would accept a former priest-child abuser into *my parish* if he had undergone psychological treatment and was being supervised by another priest." This places additional conditions on his return and brings the question home to the respondent: the priest-perpetrator will be coming into *your* parish. Participants responded as follows in Table 3 on the next page.

The change in the survey responses from the first to the second statement is important. When a priest-offender has gone through treatment and is being supervised, a majority of active Catholics would accept the man back into their own parishes. The percentage who would *not* want him back dropped from 42 percent to 22 percent. It is likely that if even more conditions were placed upon the returning priest, such as those mentioned

---

Table 3

"I would accept a former priest-child abuser into *my parish*
if he had undergone psychological treatment
and was being supervised by another priest."

Percent (%) Agreement

51	27	22
% agreement	% unsure	% disagreement

(sample N = 1,810)

---

later in this chapter, e.g., a ministry not involving minors, an increasing percentage would be supportive of his return.

Educational efforts and disseminating new data on recidivism and successes in treatment will be important, not only for our Catholic leaders, but for the general community. In addition, the data suggest that there will be increasing support from Catholics for a return to ministry for some offenders if there are conditions upon which the decision is made and strict requirements upon the priest's life and ministry.

Factors to Consider

A common but unhealthy myth regarding child molesters is that they are all the same. In fact, adults who sexually molest children are clinically and behaviorally quite different. I recall a twenty-six-year-old priest who fondled a single sixteen-year-old girl in an impulsive act. Clinically, he was a very different man from a fifty-year-old narcissistic priest who coerced and seduced scores of twelve-year-old boys. I suggest that it would be inappropriate, and hazardous, for society and the Church to deal with them in exactly the same manner.

After several years of working with Church leaders considering a return to ministry for former sex offenders, some important clinical and pastoral factors have emerged:

- *Clinical Diagnosis and Abuse History.* As noted above, Adele Mayer outlined several factors contributing to poor-

risk candidates. Priests with few of these negative indicators would likely be a better risk. For example, a priest
who abused older children, had few victims, did not use
overt violence and was without a severe character disorder
or organic brain deficits would be a better candidate for a
return to ministry. On the other hand, a priest who
abused scores of prepubescent children, sometimes em-
ploying violence, and had a serious personality disorder
would probably be a poor risk for any future ministry.

- *Quality of Treatment and Response to Treatment.* Before
  considering a return to ministry, it will be important for
  the perpetrator to have gone through and done reason-
  ably well in a program that specializes in treating sex offenders. Sometimes perpetrators are placed in therapy
  with well-intentioned counselors who are not trained in
  dealing with child molesters. These therapists can be manipulated by the offenders and may end up colluding in
  their patients' denial and projection of guilt. A skilled
  sex offenders' program will assist the patient in honestly
  acknowledging his problem, taking personal responsibility for the harm he has caused, and committing himself
  to a program of recovery. Without achieving these and
  other therapeutic goals, the perpetrator is not ready to
  re-engage in ministry. A good treatment outcome will
  be important for a return to ministry.

- *Aftercare Program.* It is vital that the perpetrator's recovery be an ongoing process that extends well beyond
  the initial treatment. Such aftercare programs are usually
  multi-year, structured, and comprehensive including ongoing individual and group therapy, regular meetings
  with a support group, and periodic assessments of
  progress. Like any mental illness, a successful recovery
  for sex offenders is a process that requires dedication and
  hard work. This comprehensive program should be in
  place and functioning before he returns to ministry.

- *Availability of Supervision and Ministry Not Involving
  Minors.* Even with a positive treatment outcome and a
  comprehensive aftercare program, I would not recom-

mend that a priest-perpetrator *ever* return to a ministry that directly involves minors. I believe it would be a pastorally imprudent decision to place the perpetrator back into a significant position of trust with minors. It will be important to find a ministry that includes a different age group and that his ministry be supervised in the external forum by someone who is aware of his background. Regular sessions with this supervisor will include frank discussions of any incidental contact with minors and related behaviors.

- *Other Pastoral Considerations.* There may be extenuating circumstances which affect the possibility of the priest's return to ministry. For example, has there been considerable public notoriety about his case? Are victims or victims' families threatening legal action if he returns to ministry? Are there a number of past victims who have not yet come forward who would be affected by seeing him in a ministerial role? These and other similar pastoral considerations must be taken into account by any bishop or superior who is deliberating the ministerial prospects of a priest-offender.

- *If Needed, Consider a Waiting Period.* Sometimes a priest has done well in treatment but the treating facility and/or the diocese believe the priest is not yet ready to return to ministry. If questions persist about the stability of his recovery, a period of one to three years of a time away from ministry might strengthen the priest's recovery and provide assurances of his perseverance. At the end of this time, his superiors might then reassess his suitability for some sort of ministry.

This list of factors is not exhaustive. In some cases, there may be additional canonical, civil, and community concerns which will instrumentally affect a bishop's or major superior's decision.

A Safer Option for Our Children?

Of paramount concern is the safety of our children. While it is understandable that some adults will react in a strong, negative way to the very thought of returning a priest-perpetrator to some form of ministry, the first concern in everyone's mind is the safety of our children.

What is safer for our children: (1) releasing a former priest-perpetrator into society unsupervised, without continuing therapy, and without restraints on child contact, or (2) placing some of them in a supervised setting, in ongoing therapy, and in a ministry not involving direct contact with minors?

Psychology cannot guarantee 100 percent that a perpetrator will not re-offend in the future. Moreover, we cannot guarantee that *any* given adult will not sexually molest a child. One might argue that the probability of re-arrest for a successfully treated and supervised priest-perpetrator (arguably less than 3 percent) is no different than the probability that any other priest will be arrested for sexually abusing minors. Sadly, there is no life without risk.

I believe it would be a pastorally prudent decision to return to a limited ministry a priest-perpetrator who does well in treatment, has few negative treatment indicators, has a comprehensive aftercare program in place, is supervised in the external forum, and who is placed in a ministry that does not involve minors. There are more than a few men who have returned and are quietly serving under these circumscribed conditions.

And all perpetrators, even those who should not return to active ministry, can enter the path of recovery.

No one, neither the victim of childhood sexual abuse, nor the perpetrator of this terrible crime, is beyond the healing power of God.

Challenge to Faith

As long as we continue to expect our priests to be better than other people and our institutional Church to respond better than secular organizations, we are set up for a great disappointment. Allegations of clerical sexual misconduct will challenge our faith. As a friend of Fr. Smith, the Baltimore priest who committed suicide, said, "In all honesty, I find the whole thing incomprehensible. It's a real test of a person's faith, let me tell you." [15]

[15]S. Shane, 22A.

Applying James Fowler's "Stages of Faith" might be helpful. In the early stages of one's faith development, religious symbols "are not separable from what they symbolize."[16] In these "conventional" stages of faith, the symbol of the priest and the institutional Church are perceived as being inseparable from the Divine. In such a faith, one would expect a priest and the religious institution to be better than others.

But when allegations of clerical sexual misconduct surface and the Church's response is less than expected, a conventional faith is threatened. There is an internal contradiction between one's expectations and reality. The feeling that often arises is one of confusion. After Fr. Smith's death, one parishioner was quoted as saying, "It just isn't making sense."[17]

A state of strong cognitive tension will not be endured for long. The believer will attempt to resolve the tension. At this point, there are three basic options: deny the truth of the allegations, leave the Church altogether, or move to a higher stage of faith.

The cleric who attended my workshop had been dealing with these allegations by denying them. He had not been faced with a crisis of faith because he rejected the truth of the allegations altogether. His faith stance had been unthreatened.

The second option, leaving the Church altogether, is another way that some have dealt with the crisis. Instead of rejecting the allegations, this group rejects the Church and its symbols. I know there are some who have chosen this option. Again, the crisis of faith is avoided, not resolved.

In order to resolve the crisis, the two conflicting realities must be juxtaposed and then synthesized into a higher resolution. The two apparently conflicting truths are: (1) "Some priests have sexually abused children and the institutional Church has not always responded well" and (2) "Priests and the institutional Catholic Church are symbols of the Divine." Can these two statements both be true?

---

[16]James W. Fowler, *Stages of Faith: The Psychology of Human Development and the Quest for Meaning* (New York: Harper & Row, 1981) 163.

[17]S. Shane, "Colleagues, parishioners distraught over St. Stephen's priest's suicide," *Baltimore Sun*, August 24, 1993.

Fowler points the way to a higher resolution. In the later stages of faith, the believer accepts that sometimes deeply flawed human beings and religious institutions can be channels of divine grace. The person of the priest and the religious institution are, at once, sinner and vessel of grace. In later stages, allegations of clerical sexual abuse or inappropriate Church response might cause the believer to be outraged and/or saddened, but they do not cause a crisis of faith.

If the community of faith and the individual believer can both move to this higher resolution, it would facilitate facing allegations of clerical sexual misconduct when they arise. Appropriate emotions such as anger and/or sadness would still accompany the revelation that a child has been abused, but the revelation might be manageable. If the faithful can manage this crisis successfully and communicate that confidence to others, I believe that the victims and the perpetrators will share in their confidence.

Clearly, the priests who commit suicide in the wake of allegations do not believe they can manage. They are overwhelmed and shamed. They are reflecting the feelings of a faith community that also feels overwhelmed and shamed. Some would like the whole problem to go away. For many, it seems like too much cognitive tension. A few of our priest-perpetrators acquiesced and went away.

But there are initial signs of hope. Many dioceses and religious orders have managed the crisis. They have responded openly and courageously. I personally know lay Catholics, men and women religious, priests and bishops who have faced this issue squarely. Their courage has helped victims and perpetrators alike come to terms with their own truth and to find healing. They have learned that they can get through this awful moment.

A Most Dangerous Time

The most dangerous time for a priest-perpetrator is immediately after being confronted. The truth comes crashing in and he may move into a state of psychic overload.

Some priests begin to conjure up the worst of scenarios. They may imagine the hatred and the derision they will receive. The prospect of scathing media coverage or the possibility of an impending trial weigh heavily. But their core struggle is within.

That fundamental conflict arises: How could I, a priest, have done such a despicable thing?

In this early stage, priest-perpetrators are likely to despair of their entire lives and ministry. They may come to believe that they have done no good in their lives and feel like utter failures. So many have told me they ardently wish they could turn back the clock and undo the damage they have done.

At this moment, they are in need of immediate support. At the time of the confrontation and at regular intervals thereafter, the bishop or superior and the priest personnel director should ask the accused priest directly how he is doing. I would not recommend that the alleged perpetrator be allowed to go on retreat or be separated from regular human contact. This can exacerbate depressive symptoms and suicidal ideation.

In addition to providing an advocate and/or therapist to assist alleged victims through the healing process, it is advisable to provide an advocate for the alleged perpetrator as well. He might be given the option to choose a priest-mentor with whom he will stay in regular contact and/or a therapist to provide interim therapeutic support until the final disposition of his situation is decided.

If the priest speaks of suicidal thoughts or feelings, or looks and/or acts seriously depressed, immediate psychotherapeutic assistance is needed. If he begins to manifest dangerous behavior and/or speaks of imminent suicidal action, a psychiatric hospitalization should be investigated.

It has happened that a priest will not manifest or admit any suicidal thoughts or behavior, yet will still be at serious risk. In one previous priest-suicide, the bishop asked the man directly if he was considering "hurting himself." The priest denied being at risk for suicide but killed himself shortly thereafter.

If the religious superiors provide consistent pastoral and therapeutic support and inquire about the priest regularly, there is little else that can be done. No one can stop a person from committing suicide if he hides suicidal intent and refuses assistance when offered. There are limits to suicide prevention.

Propelled by Faith

I believe the fact that more priests *do not* commit suicide in the face of allegations is partly because of their faith.

After working with scores of priests who have molested children, I have found many of them to suffer from significant psychological impairments. Most are bright, verbal, and sophisticated. But a closer clinical evaluation reveals psychosocial and psychosexual deficiencies. But what also has been apparent to me is their courage and their faith. Even in the face of seemingly having lost everything, they struggle in treatment to hear the truth. They challenge one another toward a rigorous honesty. And the only fuel left to propel them is their faith. I suspect that there will be a time in each of our lives when we, too, stripped of worldly supports, will have to go forward armed with only our courage and our faith. I find many of them to provide positive examples.

Each day at 8:15 A.M., the morning liturgy at Saint Luke Institute is presided over by one of our residents. Their homilies are given from the heart. These men speak of sin, forgiveness, brokenness, and healing. They know firsthand the Christian truths about repentance, sorrow, and hope. Many times these men will share their own journeys with their pains and their joys. They attempt to turn their futures, which are often murky, over to God and to trust in him.

I cannot help but think that their words are important ones to hear. I know they have been for me. I also know that it will be a long time before our society and our Church will view these men as potential sources of grace. That day may never come. It will be a loss.

A Time for Hope

To be angry and saddened by allegations of clerical-child sexual abuse is a normal and healthy reaction. Sexual abuse is a terrible crime which has serious implications for our children and our Church.

But to treat perpetrators with disgust and to single them out for derision and violence may say something more about our society than it does about these men. It is no accident that priests confronted with alcoholism, anonymous sexual encounters, or stealing from their churches do not commit suicide, but some priest-perpetrators of child abuse do. I believe that their self-destruction is an expression of the message of hatred and despair that they have received and internalized.

The time has come for a message of hope both for victims and for perpetrators of child sexual abuse. Victims can become survivors. Perpetrators can find the road to recovery.

It is important not to underestimate the trauma caused to the victims and the psychological impairments of perpetrators. It is just as important not to overlook the fact that thousands of victims of child sexual abuse have been able to recover and live happy, productive lives. There are countless perpetrators who, likewise, have found peace and inner healing, and have not re-offended. There are even some who have gone through a successful treatment program and have quietly returned to a limited ministry.

A unique gift the Christian faith has to give is the healing power of Christ. Some victims and perpetrators have availed themselves of this gift. Many more have not. There is much more work to be done.

Our most important Christian gift, however, is the gift of hope. There are many, many tragedies in this life and we will never be able to heal them all. Despair is never far from the human condition. But the gift of hope enables us to raise our heads, to look out toward the kingdom, and to hasten toward it with all speed.

Chapter Six

A Conversion of Perspective

Getting Rid of the Problem?

Some months ago, I was on the phone with a Catholic bishop in the United States discussing the subject of child sexual abuse. With a deep sigh he said, "Well, I guess this problem is not going to go away." After six years of sustained media attention, he had finally resigned himself to the idea that the issue of child sexual abuse might not be just another passing phase. The possibility that his ministerial work would continue indefinitely to include the issue of child sexual abuse was, for him, a most distressing thought.

Indeed, child sexual abuse is an ugly subject. When it involves clergy and religious as perpetrators, it is especially upsetting and distasteful. There are a lot of people, not just this Catholic bishop, who wish it would go away.

As discussed in the previous chapter, one way we are trying to make it go away is by getting rid of the perpetrators. An increasing percentage are being banned from any sort of future ministry regardless of their response to psychotherapeutic treatment. Similarly, there continues to be an ecclesiastical movement to make it easier to laicize forcibly priest-perpetrators. Our unspoken hope is that if we get rid of the men caught sexually abusing minors, the problem might simply disappear.

But even if we succeed in forcing them out of the priesthood, these perpetrators are only released without supervision into a society replete with children. The infamous re-offenses of (Fr.) James

Portions of this chapter appeared as "Child sexual abuse: a conversion of perspective," *The Tablet*, 249(8059) (January 21, 1995) 74–76.

Porter after his resignation from priesthood are cases in point. The problem is not disposed of; it simply changes clothes and venue.

One can empathize with the desire to get rid of this problem. The intensive media exposure has been devastating. Civil lawsuits have cost millions. More than a few priest-perpetrators are in jail. Victims have railed against the Church's response. Clergy morale has been hit hard. By anyone's account, the situation has been ugly, damaging, expensive, and disheartening.

Our natural inclination is to beseech the Almighty to get rid of this problem. The unspoken prayer in our heart has been, "O God, please make it go away."

But it has *not* gone away.

A Conversion Needed

There is an old proverb which speaks of it being hard to kick against the goad. A goad was a six-to-seven-foot wooden stick used to prod oxen. When oxen kicked against the goad, the prodding was all the more painful. In the Acts of the Apostles (26:14), Jesus told Paul that by persecuting the Christians, Paul was fighting the grace of God and, by analogy, kicking against the goad. He was resisting God, who cannot be thwarted, and thus made his life all the more painful.

It may be that our perspective toward the surfacing of the reality of child sexual abuse has been like kicking against the goad. If God has not heard our prayer to take the problem away, it may be because we have not been praying rightly.

Before we can ever deal with the reality of child sexual abuse in a fully Christian way, there will need to be a conversion of our perspective. Our response to the reality of child sexual abuse has not only been *negative*, it has tended to be excessively *legal, focused on offenders,* and *limited*. On the other hand, I argue that a fully Christian perspective and response should be *positive, pastoral, pro-victim,* and *proactive*.

A Positive Approach

First, our attitude toward the surfacing of allegations of child sexual abuse has been *negative*. What is needed, most of all, is a *positive* approach.

Abuse Is Long-Standing and Widespread

A large number of children suffer the effects of child sexual abuse. It is commonly thought that about one out of every three or four girls and one out of every five to eight boys in our society are sexually abused by the age of eighteen. My own recent study affirmed these numbers. Of the 1,810 active Roman Catholics in the United States and Canada who responded to the survey, 20.8 percent of the 1,234 women and 16.3 percent of the 575 men said they had been sexually molested as children.[1]

Not only is child sexual abuse widespread, it is also long-standing. In A.D. 309, the Council of Elvira's canon 71 stated, "People who sexually abuse boys shall not be given communion even at the end." In the early days of the Catholic Church, there was enough awareness and concern about the evil of child sexual abuse that it was condemned by the hierarchy. In fact, this problem was so serious that a Church law, or "canon," was promulgated to condemn it.

Nor is child sexual abuse by priests only a recent occurrence. In 1570, records from an ecclesiastical court in Florence document a case in which Luigi Fontino, a canon of the Church of Our Lady of Loreto, sodomized a choir boy, Luigi dalla Balla, who was probably around fifteen or sixteen years old. Although Fontino initially maintained his innocence, he was imprisoned in irons for two months. Under threat of torture and suggestions of leniency if he confessed, Fontino admitted the charges. He was defrocked of his priestly status, turned over to the secular authorities, and decapitated. The victim, Luigi dalla Balla was whipped and exiled from the Papal States.[2]

Similarly, in 1576 in Loreto, another choirboy alleged sexual abuse against more than one priest in the town. These priests fared better. Their goods were confiscated and they were defrocked.[3]

---

[1]There were 7,201 surveys sent out to predominantly active Catholics on Twenty-Third Publications' mailing list. There was a response rate of 25 percent. This study is discussed in more depth in chapter three.

[2]R. Sherr, "A Canon, a Choirboy, and Homosexuality in Late Sixteenth-Century Italy: A Case Study," *Journal of Homosexuality* 21(3) (1991) 1–22.

[3]Ibid., 10.

Child sexual abuse is not a new problem. People often ask, "Then why are we hearing so much about child sexual abuse today?" My answer is, "Because we are willing to listen."

Not so long ago a psychotherapist in private practice attended her first workshop on child sexual abuse. After returning home, three of her regular clients revealed that they had been sexually abused as minors. The psychotherapist thought that the timing of these revelations was not coincidental. She said, "My clients revealed to me that they had been abused because they sensed that I was finally ready to hear it." For centuries, children tried to tell us but we were not willing to listen.

Changes in society have made us ready to hear the truth. One of these changes has been an increased openness regarding sexual issues. The past twenty years have begun a public discussion of sexuality and sexual behavior. It has included such difficult topics as rape, sexual harassment, and child sexual abuse.

Similarly, many perpetrators of child sexual abuse will recount a dysfunctional sexual upbringing, including sexuality being a taboo subject in their homes. Sex was never discussed. Their dysfunctional sexual history is an outgrowth of a society which had great difficulty learning and expressing a healthy acceptance of sexuality.

A second change that has helped the subject of child sexual abuse surface is a change in our perspective of children. Simply put: *children have rights.*

I recall the words of a psychology professor who said, "The twentieth century is the 'Age of the Child.'" This century has witnessed a burgeoning of child protective laws. We now recognize that children are human beings who have inalienable rights. One of these is the right to grow up without being used for the sexual gratification of adults.

With an increasing openness about sexuality and a recognition that children inherently have civil rights, child sexual abuse is an issue whose time has come. To fight it will only make the process more difficult and more painful. It will not go away.

Child sexual abuse is a long-standing and pervasive problem. Now, we have the chance to do something positive about it. Instead of wishing allegations of child sexual abuse would go away, we might thank God that we have been given an opportunity to intervene in, and thus break, the cycle of abuse.

A Pastoral Approach

In addition to developing a *positive* perspective, the issue of child sexual abuse needs a *pastoral* presence.

Whenever a case of child sexual abuse breaks publicly, the institutional Church relies heavily on two professions: law and psychology. Because of the litigious nature of American society, and the monies at stake, attorneys often direct the Church's handling of the issue. Psychologists assist the Church in helping the perpetrator, sometimes the victims, and occasionally the affected parishes. The Church has crafted an institutional response that has tended to be *legal* and *psychological*. What has been sorely lacking is the *pastoral* dimension.

It is easy to dismiss allegations of clergy-child sexual abuse by stating that "the victims are in it for the money" or "it's just as much the victim's fault as the priest's fault." However, such rationalizations perpetuate an enduring defense against facing the problem directly, i.e., blaming the victim.

In reality, many victims have come first to the Church seeking solace and understanding, and have felt rejected. It is true that some victims have come forward with a suspicious and angry attitude. This attitude has made their encounters with Church officials difficult. However, this is to be expected. Someone who has been sexually violated by a cleric would naturally be angry and distrustful of other clerics. But the victim's natural suspiciousness and inner hurt are exacerbated when Church officials respond with legal jargon and a defensive posture.

What victims seek most of all is a Church that cares and acknowledges their pain. *It was a priest who molested them and they are asking for his Church to heal them.* It is not enough to offer to pay victims' psychotherapy costs. What victims want, most of all, is to be received with compassion and for the Church to say it is sorry. It seems like a small thing but it is not.

Recently, a victim of clerical abuse called me on the phone. She had been seeing a priest for counseling and he had sexually exploited her. During our conversation, she complained for quite some time about many things: the defensive comments by the vicar general of the diocese, the cold response of diocesan attorneys, as well as the priest-perpetrator's statement that she had seduced him. After a long discussion, she finally paused and said what was foremost on her mind. She had just spoken to the bishop and she almost cried when she said, "He didn't even say that he was sorry." More than anything else, she wanted the Church to say it was sorry.

I remember being at a parish where a pastor had been charged with child sexual abuse and was removed. The parishioners were devastated and came in large numbers to a town meeting with the diocesan chancellor. As the meeting progressed, the chancellor became more defensive and the people became angrier. Voices got louder and more shrill.

Finally, just when it seemed like the meeting would explode, the chancellor said, "I am sorry. This is a terrible thing and it should never have happened." Immediately, the atmosphere in the room changed. The tension level dropped. Voices quieted. The victims and their families heard what they needed.

An apology is a good beginning but a true pastoral response would do more. Unfortunately, so many pastoral people feel inadequate to do more. They say, "I'm not a professional. How can I deal with the problem of child sexual abuse?" They believe that psychologists are professionals and they unwittingly denigrate their own skills. They are implying that pastoral people are not equipped to help with such a complex and difficult subject.

But pastoral people are constantly giving support, advice, comfort and healing to victims of all sorts of traumas. They support the bereaved and the dying. They assist the sick and pray for their healing. They counsel the troubled and so many people who need a sympathetic ear.

These are precisely the skills needed by victims of child sexual abuse. Victims want to be heard. They are in need of prayer and healing. They need to grieve and to find inner peace. Who better to help them on this journey than a trained pastoral professional with years of experience!

It is wrong for pastoral people to claim they are not professionals. It is true that they are not psychologists and thus cannot do psychotherapy. Nor are they attorneys, so they should not talk like attorneys nor use legal jargon. Rather, they are highly trained and experienced religious professionals whose message is hope and whose language is the Sacred Scriptures.

We should greet alleged victims with compassion and concern. We should listen to the sorrow in their hearts. We should offer any assistance we are able to give. And we should leave legal and clinical judgments to others.[4]

This pastoral gift has been sometimes lacking in our approach which has been heavily weighted toward the legal and the clinical. In recent months, however, there has been an increasing awareness of the need for the Church's stance to be primarily pastoral. For example, "Restoring Trust," published by the United States NCCB, emphasized that the work of its ad hoc committee was to fashion "a pastoral response." Likewise, Church sexual abuse policies in Ireland, England and Scotland have all emphasized the Church's pastoral mission in cases of abuse. Mark Chopko, general counsel for the NCCB, summarized this progress, "We have learned that an exclusively 'legal' approach which ignores the human dimension is not the best approach."[5]

Over 1,600 years ago, the Council Fathers of Elvira spoke out against the evil of child sexual abuse in an era when using a child for sexual pleasure was accepted by many in society. Their pronouncement was an act of courage over 1,600 years before society would also raise a consistent public voice against this evil. I believe that the Church is called to give prophetic voice with the same pastoral courage in facing the issue of child sexual abuse today.

A Pro-Victim Approach

As the Church raises a positive, pastoral voice on the issue of child sexual abuse, I believe it should also be a voice that is pro-victim. While the Church has a mission to all peoples, rich and poor alike, it has a special love and a duty to serve the powerless and the poor.

Jesus spent the bulk of his ministry with the poor. They were the ones who followed him. I suspect it was they whom he loved

[4]Cf. A. J. Placa, "Legal Aspects of the Sexual Abuse of Children," in *Slayer of the Soul: Child Sexual Abuse and the Catholic Church,* ed. S. J. Rossetti (Mystic, Conn.: Twenty-Third Publications, 1990) 163–164.

[5]Mark Chopko, "Restoring Trust and Faith," in *A Brief Overview of Conference Involvement in Assisting Dioceses With Child Molestation Claims* (Washington, D.C.: NCCB's Ad Hoc Committee on Sexual Abuse, September 1993) 40.

most of all. Down through its history, the Church has had a unique love and ministry to the weak and to the poor.

We see the Catholic Church's pro-life stance and its ministry on behalf of the unborn as an example of this preferential option for the powerless and the poor. The Church is a vociferous voice on behalf of the unborn, condemning the evil of abortion. Fetuses are powerless to speak for themselves so the Church rightly becomes their voice.

It is my firm belief that we will never truly be a Church on the issue of child sexual abuse until we become the voice of the victims. While the Church must be concerned with the welfare of the perpetrators, their parishes, and the good of the overall Church, it is victims and victims' groups where the Church's heart should be.

The institutional Church has been struggling mightily to develop response policies when allegations of sexual abuse arise. Although we might end up fashioning good response policies and executing just settlements, these only put us on a par with a fair secular institution. If we only go this far, we still will not have become a Church.

It is our calling to speak on behalf of children who are being sexually abused. They are too small and too powerless to speak for themselves. Someone must be their mouthpiece and their champion. It is a natural role for the followers of Jesus to take up this mantle. It is a particularly suitable role for the Roman Catholic Church; advocating for abused children is a natural extension of its pro-life stance.

Unfortunately, we see the Church today locked in a public struggle with victims. For example, in America, victims' groups such as SNAP and the LINKUP often are at odds with the Church institution in the media and in our legal courts. Victims are pitted against bishops, religious superiors, and dioceses. The conflict is played out on the television, in the newspapers, and in civil trials. Not only is it financially costly and damaging to the trust Catholics have in their Church, this conflict is inherently contrary to what the victims truly want and what the Church should be.

Most victims, in their heart of hearts, want the Church to care for them and to be on their side. People in society expect the Church to be the voice of the victims, not the recipient of their civil lawsuits.

A partnership between victims' groups and the Church hierarchy will require nothing less than a change of heart, a conversion, for both victims and Church. Instead of meeting alleged victims with skepticism and closed doors, the Church's gospel stance toward them is a pair of open arms and a pastoral spirit. Instead of victims viewing Church leaders with suspicion, their true desire is for acceptance and support.

Perhaps this is idealistic—to expect an institution to receive warmly a person who alleges that one of its leaders has perpetrated sexual abuse. Is it also too much to hope for victims to allow the Church to become their advocate? Many victims and their organizations are reluctant to see the good will of so many bishops and religious leaders on this issue. The Church must go beyond defensive institutional impulses to realize its true nature. And victims will only fully live in peace when they have opened themselves to a healing of spirit in the Church.

The day when the Catholic Church sits on the same side of the table as the victims of child sexual abuse and becomes their advocate is the day when it has truly become a Church on this issue. There are, indeed, signs of hope. Jeanne Miller, founder of the victims' group, the LINKUP, has spent considerable time in dialogue with members of the hierarchy. Likewise, Bishop Kinney and his staff of the ad hoc committee have repeatedly reached out to the LINKUP, SNAP, and other victims of clergy-child sexual abuse. Although progress has been made in this dialogue, there is much to be done.

A Proactive Approach

In addition to fashioning a perspective that is *positive, pastoral,* and *pro-victim,* we will ultimately want to respond to the reality of child sexual abuse in a *proactive* way.

The Catholic Church and our society are trying to develop good response policies once an allegation of child sexual abuse occurs. With every state in the Union having a child abuse reporting statute and just about every Catholic diocese having a response policy, leaders are beginning to sit back and say, "We have done our job." Indeed, we have made a good beginning, but we have not yet finished our work.

If so many young people in society are sexually abused by the age of eighteen, shouldn't we wonder why so many are being abused and try to do something to heal the problem at its root?

A Distortion of Sexuality and Aggression

In my book, *Slayer of the Soul: Child Sexual Abuse and the Catholic Church,* I argued that child sexual abuse is a perversion of the natural impulses of sexuality and aggression. I also argued that these distortions are not present solely in the perpetrators of child sexual abuse but are found in the very marrow of our society. To address proactively the evil of child sexual abuse, we must go beyond treating the offending adults and treat a society whose own deviancy has spawned this tragedy.

Robert Stoller put forth the notion that all sexual deviances were a manifestation of an "eroticized hatred." Following this lead, I said that the widespread sexual abuse of children in our society is a reflection of our society's distorted perceptions of the human impulses of sexuality and aggression.

Some have said that child sexual abuse, like rape, is only a crime of aggression and that it has nothing to do with sexuality. I disagree. If it were only about aggression, why do not perpetrators simply hit their victims over the head with a wrench? They do not. Rather, their aggressive act of touching a child, through the mystery of human sexuality, becomes an erotic moment. The act of child sexual abuse is both aggressive and sexual.

Child sexual abuse is an abuse of sexuality. Child sexual abuse is also an act of aggression. If we are to heal this illness at its root, there are fundamental changes needed in society's understanding of sexuality and in its expression of human aggression.

An Abuse of Power

But I have come to realize that healing our sexual and aggressive deviances will not be enough. There is yet another essential ingredient to the reality that is child sexual abuse. More than an abuse of sexuality and an act of aggression, child sexual abuse is also *a misuse of power.*

Research suggests that the most traumatizing element of sexual abuse for children is not the fact of their being used as a sexual object. Rather, the most damaging element is the abuse of human trust and thus, the abuse of power. The child was in a vulnerable position, i.e., the adult was given power over the child. This power was to be used for the child's good. Instead, it was abused.

I remember treating a Scout leader who had sexually abused several twelve-year-old boys. Normally, a passive and downcast man, he "lit up" and became quite animated when speaking about his relationships with these young males. I asked him, "How do you feel when you are with these boys?" He answered, "It makes me feel strong." When an adult only feels powerful with children, acts of child abuse are not far behind.

An abuse of power is also evident in clergy-child sexual abuse. In an extreme example, one Canadian mother revealed that the pastor of her parish had telephoned one morning at 3:00 A.M. and asked for her son to be sent to the rectory to assist the priest. She dutifully woke her son who went to the rectory where he was molested by the pastor. Not only was this an abuse of power, but one suspects that the power this pastor wielded over his parishioners was regularly abusive to many people, not just to children.

Sometimes people speculate that men with a sexual attraction to children might be drawn to the priesthood because of its requirement of celibacy. I suspect it is just as likely that some pedophiles are drawn to the priesthood because of the power the priest can wield.

The psychological treatment of child sexual abuse essentially includes a healthy empowerment of the perpetrators. Formerly, perpetrators found their "strength" by abusing the powerless. Now, they are to find a mature sense of power by a realization of their own competence and efficacy as adults.

Likewise, if we are to become proactive in our treatment of the issue of child sexual abuse, we will necessarily rethink the way our society, and our Church, understand and exercise power. If we are to heal our society *before* it creates a climate that spawns the sexual abuse of children, we must heal our own broken sense of power and our grasping for control in violent and abusive ways.

This is a Herculean task. But if child sexual abuse is a widespread and long-standing societal disease, then the antidote must be equally pervasive.

Perhaps it will never occur. Truly, the abuse of power and its sequelae, acts of child sexual abuse, are rooted in deeply buried flaws in the human character. But there is a way.

A New Vision of Power

Within the Gospels themselves is the answer to these questions and to the dilemma of power. Power struggles are as old as the Scriptures. At one point, the disciples began arguing among themselves about who was the greatest. Jesus responded, "and said, 'Amen, I say to you, unless you turn and become like children, you will not enter the kingdom of heaven'" (NAB Matt 18:3). Jesus also admonished his disciples not to become like "earthly kings": "He said to them, 'The kings of the Gentiles lord it over them and those in authority over them are addressed as "Benefactors"'" . . . (NAB Luke 22:25).

Rather, they, like the Son of Man, should use their authority to serve. As a sign of this service, Jesus washed the feet of his disciples at the Last Supper. He told them, "If I, therefore, the master and teacher, have washed your feet, you ought to wash one another's feet" (NAB John 13:14).

And the ultimate sign of service was Jesus' death. Instead of using his power to establish an earthly kingdom, he submitted himself to a humble death. Through this willing powerlessness came the greatest healing.

Without the heart of a child and a spirit of service, there will continue to be abuses of power on every level of our society, including the sexual abuse of our children. Yet, there are already signs of hope emerging.

For example, the cardinal primate of Ireland, Cardinal Daly, has himself begun to take a more open and courageous stance on this issue. In recent media appearances, he has spoken of his anger and outrage when learning that children had been sexually abused by priests. He has been brought to tears over the damage it has caused and he has vowed to cooperate fully with the civil authorities. On Irish radio he said, "We are humbled by the whole experience."

Whatever vestiges were left of a triumphal Church after Vatican II are being shattered by recent allegations of clergy-child sexual abuse. In the wake of this destruction is a more humble Church, committed to serve.

Expensive Grace

In August of 1994, Abbot Timothy Kelly and the Benedictines at Saint John's Abbey in Collegeville, Minnesota, hosted the annual LINKUP conference for victims of clergy sexual abuse. It was an act of courage. There had been several highly publicized incidents of monks from the abbey sexually abusing children. The presence of these victims of clergy-child sexual abuse at the abbey were a painful reminder of the abbey's past.

At the end of the conference, Abbot Kelly was invited to address the participants. He graciously thanked them for coming to Saint John's. The abbot said their presence had been an "expensive grace." It had "cost" them much; it had been very painful. But it had also been a moment of healing and reconciliation for his community. He recognized, within this difficult moment, the hidden work of God.

I believe the surfacing of the long-hidden reality of child sexual abuse is, indeed, the work of God. The time is right. We have been given a sacred task to assist in this work. We are to break the cycle of child sexual abuse.

If we fall into a negative and limited response, we will be kicking against the goad and each step taken will be all the more painful. But if we approach this terrible reality with a perspective that is *positive, pastoral, pro-victim,* and *proactive,* we will be far along the road to recovery.

We are in a painful and yet grace-filled time. I believe this is the work of God's Spirit and it will not be thwarted. Changes will and must come. We will become a humbler Church. It is an important grace and it will cost us much. But it has always been thus with any conversion to humility.

Chapter Seven
Silver Lining in a Dark Cloud

A Cover-Up?

Many have accused the hierarchy of the Catholic Church with covering up incidents of clergy-child sexual abuse. There has been an oft-made innuendo that Catholic bishops have maliciously determined to bury cases of clergy-sexual misconduct. These charges have escalated to the point where an American diocese has been accused of violating the Rico Act, a statute used against the racketeering and conspiracy of organized crime. The Church has been accused of engaging in an organized conspiracy of shielding priest-perpetrators of child sexual abuse from the law.

I have not seen evidence of an organized conspiracy. My experience is that most bishops have been deeply concerned with instances of child sexual abuse and have responded as well as they were able. Despite this good will, however, many shocking errors have been made.

Part of the problem lies in a lack of information. As the Church learns more, its response to allegations of sexual misconduct by clergy has been improving. But there are deeper realities involved.

Portions of this chapter appeared as: Stephen J. Rossetti, "Child Sexual Abuse in the Church: How I Understand It," *The Priest* 50(1) (January 1994) 32–37.

A Clash of Cultures

I believe that our sometimes inadequate response to child sexual abuse is also a result of fundamental conflicts between the Catholic Church and Western society. America, for example, is an open and fast-paced culture that expects a decisive and rapid reaction. When allegations of child sexual abuse surfaced in Fall River, Massachusetts, in May of 1992, the case of (Fr.) James Porter quickly became national news. American Catholics wanted to know what was happening and what the Church intended to do.

However, unlike the fast-paced American culture, the Catholic Church is slow. It charts a cautious, determined course. As one archbishop said, "The Catholic church thinks in terms of centuries." The first public case of clergy-child sexual abuse broke in 1985 in Louisiana with Fr. Gilbert Gauthe; a full eight years later, in 1993, the American bishops convened an ad hoc committee and began to investigate publicly the problem.

Not only is the Church slow to react, the Church is discreet to the point of appearing secretive. The Catholic Church culture makes every effort to maintain confidentiality, especially with sensitive information. Potential scandals are kept from public view. As a result, early deliberations on clergy-child sexual abuse by the American bishops were held in *closed* session.

When the open, fast-paced Western culture met the closed, slow-moving culture of the Catholic Church in the arena of child sexual abuse, the results were predictable. As one reporter said, "The silence of the church is deafening." The media have consistently accused the Church of a cover-up.

Church officials, on the other hand, felt unjustly accused and distrusted. They could not understand why people did not see how concerned the bishops were nor appreciated all that the Church hierarchy had done. But the bishops had done it behind closed doors.

I do not fault people for being upset with the bishops' slow response. Nor do I fault bishops for dealing with this problem in the same manner that they have always dealt with potential scandals.

A New Openness

However, the time has come for us, as a Church, to change. We can no longer think "in terms of centuries" when a crisis like sexual misconduct by clergy strikes. Such moments call for clear, decisive, and visible leadership.

In fact, the American bishops' approach is slowly changing. In November 1992, they passed a resolution on clergy sexual misconduct which signaled a change. They resolved, "Within the confines of respect for the privacy of the individuals involved, deal as openly as possible with members of the community." In June of 1993, their first *open* general session on child sexual abuse was convened, with media invited.

The transition to a more open and responsive stance will be a difficult one for the Catholic Church. It has long emphasized discretion and caution in dealing with its problems. The pressure of our open and fast-paced Western society is slowly effecting a change in the Church. When there are incidents of clergy-child sexual abuse, a swift and open response is imperative.

Priesthood in Transition

Because of incidents of clerical sexual misconduct, many priests and more than a couple of bishops are privately wondering if the priesthood has become corrupt. Tom Fox gave voice to this dark fear in a *New York Times* editorial. Among other trends, he cited incidents of clergy-child sexual abuse and sexually active priests. Fox said the clerical order may be "in a state of collapse."[1]

Despite the lack of empirical statistics, my clinical experience suggests that approximately 2 to 7 percent of Catholic clergy are sexually involved with minors at some point in their priestly lives. While this is a terrible reality, these men are still a small minority of the priesthood.

Many people ask how this figure of 2 to 7 percent compares with the general population of males. The answer is, "We do not know." One might make an educated guess based on a study by Briere and Runtz. They interviewed 193 male undergraduates concerning these students' sexual interest in children. The study found that 9 percent of the sample admitted some sexual fantasies involving children, 5 percent said they had masturbated to

---

[1]Thomas C. Fox, "Wrong About Sex, Absolutely," *New York Times,* July 16, 1993.

these sexual fantasies, and 7 percent indicated there was some likelihood of having sex with children if they thought they would not be caught.[2] The percentage of priests sexually involved with children probably approximates the males in our society who are also sexually interested in children.

Priesthood Exposed

Tom Fox thought that "a good number of priests . . . admit to sexual activity." He found this another reason to suggest the priesthood is collapsing. However, sexual activity by vowed celibates is not a new phenomenon. In A.D. 309, the Council of Elvira promulgated canon 18 which stated:

> Bishops, presbyters, and deacons, if—once placed in the ministry—they are discovered to be sexual offenders, shall not receive communion, not even at the end, because of the scandal and the heinousness of the crime.[3]

What may be new is that, in our open and sexually explicit society, the sexual activity of secular and religious leaders is *publicly exposed*. It is also progress that we have moved beyond the harshness of the council's canons on sexuality.

Older priests can remember when civil authorities cooperated with Church leaders to keep the image of the priesthood untarnished. Cases of priestly misconduct were often handled behind closed doors. It was expected that the bishop would deal with clerical problems according to Church law and it was unusual to disclose such events to the media. Even if the media became aware of priestly misconduct, they rarely reported the incident.

This is true not only of our priests, but of other leaders and professionals in our society as well: doctors, judges, senators, and congressmen. There was an unspoken agreement that the public image of these professions was important to maintain.

---

[2]J. Briere and M. Runtz, "University Males' Sexual Interest in Children: Predicting Potential Indices of 'Pedophilia' in a Nonforensic Sample," *Child Abuse and Neglect* 13 (1989) 65.

[3]Samuel Laeuchli, *Power and Sexuality* (Philadelphia: Temple University Press, 1972) 128.

But the attitude towards its leaders, including Catholic priests, has changed. Where we once hid their personal transgressions from public exposure, these sins are now broadcast for all to see. In fact, incidents of misconduct on the part of our leaders are particularly newsworthy.

Do these realities mean that the priesthood is collapsing? Perhaps. We can certainly say that a previous style of priesthood is collapsing. At the same time that the Church is becoming more open in its dealings with society, the conduct of its priests is also becoming more open to public scrutiny.

A Changing Balance of Power

The priesthood is in transition. There are forces at work in our Church that are exerting strong pressures on the priesthood. The willingness of society to air allegations of clergy sexual misconduct is only part of these larger forces at work. Accompanying this move to openness is a changing balance of power.

The Winter Commission investigated incidents of clergy-child sexual abuse in the Archdiocese of Saint John in Newfoundland. They identified underlying factors that contributed to clergy involvement in child molestation and the poor response of the archdiocese. One of these factors was the unchecked authority of the priests over the people. They repeated one of the testimonies given to the commission:

> The power, status, prestige, and lack of accountability at the parish level in particular, may have created a climate in which the insecure, power-hungry, or the deviant believed they could exploit and abuse victims with immunity from discovery or punishment.[4]

The commission agreed with this testimony. They said that this "pattern of power has not been good." It gave the Church and the priest "too much influence, unchecked by social . . .

---

[4]G. A. Winter, F. O'Flaherty, N. P. Kenny, E. MacNeil, and J. A. Scott, *The Report of the Archdiocesan Commission of Enquiry into the Sexual Abuse of Children by Members of the Clergy* (St. John's, Newfoundland: Archdiocese of St. John's, 1990) 1:92.

balances. It also precluded a healthy scepticism about some of the men who occupied positions of authority in the Church."[5]

Catholic priests have not been sufficiently accountable to the people they serve. Many priests with personality and behavioral disorders have been able to offend and hurt their parishioners with virtual impunity.

Parishioners have often felt powerless. They responded in the only ways left to them: some reduced their donations to the Church. Others simply left. Finally, after years of discontent, the priest may have been moved to another parish to begin the cycle anew.

Since the Second Vatican Council, there has been a slow shift in power from the hierarchy to the laity. Parish councils have emerged. Lay pastoral associates have engaged in regular, paid parochial ministry. The expertise of the laity is being consulted increasingly in ecclesiastical decisions. I believe the phenomenon of public awareness of clergy sexual misconduct will escalate this shift in power.

In Ireland, Bishop Forristal echoed this insight at a gathering of Church leaders on the issue of child sexual abuse. He said, "Some of us will have to make a lot of changes in the way we do things . . . we have to look at our model of church." Bishop Forristal went on to emphasize three words: "collaboration, openness, accountability."

My survey results show that the perceptions of clergy are slowly changing, particularly in response to cases of clergy-child sexual abuse. As reported earlier, there was an 11 percent drop in the expectation by laity in an affected parish that a priest's moral conduct should be better than other people's conduct. In the same group, there was a 15 percent increase in wondering if a new priest is someone they can trust. There was a 7 percent decline in looking to priests for moral leadership.

Whatever was left of the previous exalted view the laity had of Catholic priests is even more rapidly eroding in the wake of recent public allegations of clergy sexual misconduct. Their sometimes broken humanity is in full view. A little skepticism is a healthy thing.

---

[5]Ibid., 3:14.

The Catholic laity has tolerated the foibles of priests for centuries. This is changing. They will *not* tolerate priests who sexually molest children. Nor will they tolerate hesitancy on the part of the hierarchy in dealing with child abuse. I believe the laity will become less tolerant, in general, of the psychological deviancies of priests. They will insist on a greater voice in who stays in the rectory and who goes.

While the Catholic Church has always been wary of allowing parishioners to hire and fire pastors, as in many Protestant denominations, the Winter Commission suggested that the power has moved too far away from the laity. The phenomenon of clergy-child sexual abuse is likely to aid in this balancing of power between Catholic hierarchy and laity.

I believe it to be a positive outcome. The laity needs the clergy to challenge them to lead a virtuous life. It is also true that the clergy needs the laity to call them to accountability.

The new priesthood will be more responsible and responsive to the people it serves. Instead of looking down at the laity, the clergy and laity will interact eye to eye. The Church will not only preach to the laity, it will also listen.

A Painful Transition

Nevertheless, I cannot say this transition is not painful. The Catholic Church, and priests especially, are suffering. Recently, a newly ordained priest stood up in front of a community gathering and spoke of his pain; he felt ashamed to be seen in public and identified as a priest. In a similar instance, a bishop admitted that he hesitated to be seen wearing clerical garb on an airplane because of public allegations of clergy-child abuse.

The Canadian Winter Commission repeated one of the testimonials it received, "The recent events put all priests under a cloud of spoken or silent suspicion. . . . The Roman collar, once worn with pride, is now becoming a source of embarrassment and suspicion."[6] Gone are the days when priests, simply because they wore a collar, were automatically revered and trusted.

[6]Ibid., 1:viii.

Broken Symbols

Child sexual abuse is a heinous crime. When a Catholic priest is accused of misconduct, there is another dimension added—the dimension of the *sacred*. Priesthood is a sacred symbol. The theologian Paul Tillich spoke of the importance of such symbols and noted that these symbols point beyond themselves to the "source of all holiness."

Tillich suggested that people hold tenaciously to their religious symbols and "resist, often fanatically, any attempt to introduce an element of uncertainly by 'breaking the symbol,' namely, by making conscious its symbolic character."[7] Whenever the flawed humanity of a priest is revealed, the symbolic character of the priesthood is made conscious and the symbol may be broken.

The intense media coverage over the past several years revealing incidents of misconduct by priests may be breaking the symbol of the priesthood. Most recently, the Catholic Church in the United States, Canada, Austria, Ireland, Australia, and other nations around the globe has been reeling from highly publicized and costly incidents of child sexual abuse by clergy. Few dioceses have been spared the trauma and scathing media attention of one of its priests being accused. Some parish Catholics have experienced the especially painful reality of their own parish priest being charged.

For some, this will cause no crisis of faith. The extensive media coverage of clergy misconduct cases during the past several years and their own faith journeys have enabled them to reconcile two diametrically opposed concepts—a religious symbol committing a heinous crime.

But for others, still on the road to a more seasoned faith, incidents of child sexual abuse by clergy will cause an internal, psychic conflict—a cognitive dissonance. This may cause them to go through a period of questioning their faith. They may even decide it is necessary to leave the Catholic Church.

But for those who stay, a "conventional" faith, as described by James Fowler, is difficult, if not impossible, to maintain. In conventional faith, religious symbols "are not separable from what

---

[7]Paul Tillich, *Dynamics of Faith* (New York: Harper & Row, 1957) 51.

they symbolize."[8] This is the stage of faith that arises in adolescence. But, "for many adults, it becomes a permanent place of equilibrium."[9]

In recent days, incidents of clergy-child sexual abuse have challenged this equilibrium. To remain in our Catholic community, a more complex awareness must emerge. In these later stages of faith, we become "alive to paradox and the truth in apparent contradiction."[10] We understand that our symbols are frail and broken. Yet, we also accept them as channels of divine grace.

When something or someone important to us dies, we must mourn the loss. Images and ideals of priesthood to which many of us committed ourselves are being burst asunder. This is a loss. I think it would be a healthy act for us to acknowledge our loss and to grieve.

Foundational vs. Transitory Morale

This painful transition is affecting priests themselves; it is causing a drop in morale. But the results of my study suggest that this drop is probably a transitory phenomenon. It is a decline in what I call *transitory morale*. On the other hand, there is a more fundamental sense of identity and affiliation, a *foundational morale*, which, among priests, appears to be getting stronger.

The survey presented a number of statements about priesthood and Church to the 314 priests. When given the hypothetical statement, "If I had a son, I would be pleased if he wanted to be a priest," 93.6 percent of the priests agreed. Asked to rate the quality of priests we are getting today compared to the past, 71.2 percent thought the quality was about the same or better. When asked if today's Church is better or worse than the Church of the past, 70.1 percent thought today's Church was better.

The priests were given two statements concerning their general level of satisfaction: "Overall, I am satisfied with the priests that we have in the Church today"; and "Overall, I am satisfied

[8]James W. Fowler, *Stages of Faith: The Psychology of Human Development and the Quest for Meaning* (New York: Harper & Row, 1981) 163.
[9]Ibid., 172.
[10]Ibid., 198.

with the Catholic Church today." A large majority, 78.8 percent, was satisfied with the priests, and a similar percentage, 72.5 percent, was satisfied with the Church.

While the transitory morale of priests is suffering, their underlying contentment with today's priesthood and Church, i.e., their foundational morale, is strong. I believe that if we continue to exercise determined leadership to face sexual misconduct issues directly, and to effect changes in the priesthood, our transitory morale will return to a positive level. As this happens, the current downturn in morale will not be ultimately detrimental to the more significant foundational morale.

A Critical Moment in History

When I began as a therapist, one of my first clients was an elderly priest. He had many neurotic complaints: he suffered from bouts of depression and attacks of anxiety. Despite his many difficulties, he had lived a productive and courageous life. I was surprised to learn that some seventy years ago he himself had been sexually molested by a priest.

The sexual abuse of children is *not* new. What *is* new is our belief in the rights of children and our awareness of the psychic harm done to these young victims. Also new is our increasing understanding of the mental illness that spawns pedophilia and ephebophilia.

A Sacred Task

Many priests and bishops view the current clergy sexual misconduct scandals as a demonic force out to destroy the Church. I do not. If there have been any demonic forces at work, they have been the acts of child sexual abuse themselves and the secrecy that hid them.

What I see at work now is grace. We have been given the opportunity to recognize and confront an evil that has always been among us. This grace has come to us through the media, the law courts, and the victims themselves. Ultimately, it is the people of God who are demanding a change.

In A.D. 309, the Council of Elvira condemned the evil of child sexual abuse. It failed to effect a change. Where the council failed, I pray that we do not.

It is my conviction that we have been given a sacred task. We are at a unique moment in history in which we can address the sickness of child sexual abuse within the priesthood and within society. If we are able to address sexual deviancy openly and courageously, a stronger priesthood will emerge.

It would be facile to respond to the current tragedies by citing the fact that the Church has suffered and endured much in past centuries and has made it through these crises; therefore, we will traverse this tragedy as well. While it is undoubtedly true that the faith will continue, this statement glosses over the considerable psychological and spiritual harm that has been and is still being done.

While the faith itself will survive, this does not obviate the need for our concerted effort to confront child sexual abuse in the society and in our Church. It also does not excuse us from making painful changes in the priesthood so that it continues to be responsive and responsible to the people it serves.

The Hand of God

While these are painful days, I sense God's hand in these events. Rather than fighting the revelations and changes that are taking place, it is my hope that we will do all we can to bring these graces to fruition.

My own ministry has been primarily one to priests, especially to those who have been psychologically wounded. Many of them have abused children. It has been sad to see a brother priest in such inner turmoil, shame, and sometimes, denial. It has been difficult to realize how much agony he has inflicted upon others and upon the Church.

Working with wounded priests has changed me. I am not the priest I was when I began this work. I do not know if it has made me a better priest or if it has wounded me, too. Perhaps it has done a little of both.

I think it would be healthy for us all to hope that something new, even better, will emerge from these terrible days. I think it would be right to hope that this would give birth to a new incarnation of the Church. I have hope that the Church is becoming more like it was intended to be—humble, poor, willing to serve. If a better Church does emerge, it will have been a most tragic grace.